# ONE UNITED HARVEST

*Creative Recipes from America's*
*Community Supported Farms*

COLLECTED BY JULIE SOCHACKI

PHOTOGRAPHY BY JASON HOUSTON

Julie Sochacki
P.O. Box 333
New Hartford, CT 06057

www.farmcookbook.com

Cover and divider page photography and design
Copyright © 2005 Jason Houston / www.jasonhouston.com

Layout design Copyright © 2005 Morris Press Cookbooks

ISBN 0-9768599-0-4

A product of typensave™ software.

Copyright © 2005
Morris Press Cookbooks

Printed in the U.S.A. by

P.O. Box 2110 • Kearney, NE 68848
800-445-6621 • www.morriscookbooks.com

65106-ds    2

# Dedication

This book is dedicated to all who strive to create an economically feasible, ecologically sound, and socially just local and sustainable agricultural system. May this generation's hard work and perseverance help future generations create sustainable food practices in every community, available to all people. May the practice of consuming locally grown produce become simply second nature.

# Appreciation

Thank you to my husband Chris and to my two little boys for rearranging their lives and sacrificing for me so that this book could become a reality.

Thank you to my husband and to my mom for proofing the book repeatedly along with me to ensure that all the recipes are presented in their best form.

Thank you to my dad for providing me with the most optimum computer and printer for the job along with his countless hours of free entertainment for my boys.

Thank you to my parents and to Chris' parents, "my other parents," for supporting me in so many ways through all my endeavors.

Thank you to Jason Houston who went above and beyond simply designing a front cover for this book. His input and talents have been an invaluable resource to me. His time and commitment to this project and to the local and sustainable agricultural movement are commendable.

Thank you to my family, especially my mother, Nonny and Poppy, my Aunt Suzanne and my Aunt Jo. Each instilled a love of cooking into me at a very young age. As I look back to my early days of the marinara sauces, the Italian cream cakes, the sausage breads, and the "flat chicken," I realize that these dishes were all worth my time and experimentation, as they have shaped me into the cook I am today.

# A Special Thank You

A heart-felt thank you to everyone who contributed to this project.

You entrusted me with your recipes and the willingness to spread the word of your individual time-tested "kitchen secrets" across the country. All of the recipes in this book are creative and inviting ways to use fresh locally grown produce, making this cookbook an excellent resource for all who love cooking with fresh vegetables and fruits.

It was easy for you to share your methods and techniques, because this is what you, as a group, do best. Farmers, you share your harvest each and every growing season with others. Your personal sacrifices and long work hours make your community's quality of life better. Members, you make a commitment each growing season to financially support your farm. You also volunteer your time at the farm in various ways, and ensure that the greatest benefit comes from the farm's harvest.

With this in mind, I suppose it was only natural for all of you to be so giving when you received my call for help with this country-wide CSA project. Thank you for your interest and enthusiasm to come together as a group, from Maine to Hawaii and from Long Island to California. You are the reasons why this project lives up to its title: **One United Harvest**.

Julie

# A Word About CSA Farms

Who doesn't love the taste and smell of freshly picked, farm-grown vegetables; just like the type you find at a roadside farm stand on a curvy, scenic country road during a weekend drive? Who wants to wonder if the produce in your refrigerator is free of pesticides and diseases as a consequence of improper handling and storage?   Such concerns are some of what drive the Community Supported Agriculture ("CSA") movement, and why so many strongly believe in this cause.

A CSA is a relationship between a local farmer and the CSA's members.   In exchange for paying an annual fee to the farm, members are provided a weekly "share" or portion of the farmer's harvest, consisting of the fresh produce or other goods produced by the farm that week.

"Share" is a well-suited word, because "share" is what a CSA and its members do.  They share in the responsibility of promoting and securing the local farm's stability, while also sharing in the comfort of knowing the origins of your family's food, and that your family really will eat "well" tonight.

If you haven't already done so, make a healthy change for your family; join a CSA. Buy locally grown produce. Your family and your local farmers will thank you.

# A Word About The Recipes

In my own experiences as a cook, I fail miserably at following exact recipes to the "T." Instead I love to read a recipe and then experiment. I follow my senses as I cook, finding it almost impossible not to "sample" as I prepare a dish. Without using my senses, I feel left in the dark as to the outcome of my meal.

It is evident that those who contributed to make this book an outstanding resource, love the art of cooking and preparing their produce. Some recipes contain exact amounts for each ingredient, while others leave the amounts up to the cook's own preference, sharing only the ingredients themselves.

I challenge you all to follow your senses as you embark on a journey through this extraordinary recipe collection. Let your senses be your guide as you touch the produce to determine its maturity, adding more of what is ripe to your feast. Hear the snapping of a bean or the sizzle of olive oil. Smell your fare to detect the food's doneness. Taste your dish and proceed by adding more or less of any one ingredient. And finally, see the exquisite colors of the harvest in your creation. Use more or less of the ingredients in season, to make these recipes truly your own.

**Julie Sochacki**, a Connecticut native, is a mother, wife, daughter and friend. She is also an educator of children and adults as well as an avid home cook. As a mother of two young children, the importance of a holistic approach to food and the environment has taken on a whole new meaning for her. She hopes that her small contribution to society is reaching out to others in an effort to spread the word about the benefits of the local and sustainable agricultural movement. She collaborated with farms to create *One United Harvest* as a means to accomplish her goal. Julie and her family are members of Maple View Farm in Harwinton, Connecticut. Her website is www.farmcookbook.com.

**Jason Houston** is documentary photographer and graphic designer based in Great Barrington, Massachusetts. His work explores social and environmental themes and for the past five years he has been working on documenting the local and sustainable farming movement in his home region of western New England. His images have been used by The New York Times Sunday Magazine, Orion Magazine, Time Magazine, NewFarm.org, YES! Magazine, The Sierra Club, The DeCordova Museum, the Organic Gardener, and many other editorial, educational, non-profit, commercial, and fine art clients. His first solo exhibition was in 1996 in Santa Barbara, California and he is currently preparing a new exhibition on the farmers of the local and sustainable agricultural movement for a show in New York City in late 2005/early 2006. He is a member of Indian Line Farm (one of the first CSAs in the U.S.) and eats locally produced food whenever possible. His website is www.jasonhouston.com.

# Table of Contents

# A HARVEST OF VEGGIES

# A HARVEST OF VEGGIES

## TURKISH BORSCHT

### (A satisfying way to use all of your veggies.)

1 T. olive oil
1 onion, chopped
2 leeks, chopped
4 garlic cloves, minced
1 bunch beets, peeled and
chopped
2 lbs. red or green cabbage,
coarsely chopped (about 2
cups)
1-½ c. chopped celery
1-½ c. chopped carrots
3 medium potatoes, scrubbed
and diced
1-2 green peppers, seeded and
diced

4 tomatoes or 1 (14 oz.) can of
tomatoes, chopped
2 qts. water, chicken broth or
vegetable broth
salt and pepper, to taste
2 tsp. crushed dill seed
1 bunch of beet greens or small
bunch of Swiss chard,
chopped
juice of one large lemon
3 T. snipped fresh dill
1 c. plain yogurt for garnish

Sauté onion, leeks and garlic in oil until soft. Add all other vegetables except beet greens. Cook, stirring for 5 minutes. Add water or broth and bring to boil. Add salt, pepper and dill seed. Simmer one hour, covered. Stir in chopped beet greens or chard during the last 15 minutes of cooking. Stir in lemon juice, fresh dill and adjust seasonings. Serve each bowl topped with a spoon of yogurt.

Trish Mumme
Garden Patch Produce CSA
Alexandria, Ohio

# SHELLEY'S EASY VEGGIE FRY
(What a colorful display!)

| | |
|---|---|
| olive oil | eggplant |
| garlic | potatoes |
| onion | broccoli |
| tomatoes | cabbage |
| peppers | carrots |
| squash | fresh herbs |
| corn | |

In a skillet, add olive oil, garlic and onion. Sauté for 3 to 5 minutes. Add your choice of in-season veggies and sauté until tender.

**Recipe Note:** Mix with warm pasta and top with cheese!

Shelley Squier & Mike Donnelly
Squier Squash & Donnelly Farms
North English, Iowa

*"Food is the vehicle, community is the destination."*
*Jay Martin, Provident Farm, Maryland*

65106-05

# MID-SUMMER VEGGIE MELT
## (Improvise with whatever veggies you have on hand!)

1 unsliced seeded Lavain loaf, cut 3 x lengthwise, or bread of your choice
pesto, fully prepared (see the Herbs and Seasoning Vegetables chapter for recipe)
tomatoes
cheese, grated or shredded
hot and sweet peppers
onions
zucchini
fresh basil leaves
fresh pressed garlic

Place bread slices onto a cookie sheet. Spread each slice with pesto. Cover completely with thin slices of tomatoes and sprinkle with cheese. Arrange assortment of sliced veggies and cover with another layer of the sliced tomatoes and place a leaf or two of the fresh basil upon each tomato slice. Sprinkle on more cheese and drop small bits of the pressed garlic all around. Bake at 375 degrees until slightly browned.

**Recipe Note:** This is served most often on Wednesday afternoons, the day the CSA shares are packed out. It is a favorite among the members because it is tasty and a filling colorful feast on a long busy day. -Gail

Gail Kuhns
Peach Valley CSA
Silt, Colorado

# CHRISTINE POPPER'S ROASTED VEGGIES

## (The smell of the roasted veggies is fabulous!)

patty pan squash (cut
  crosswise to make fluted
  pieces)
zucchini (cut in rounds)
tomatoes
onion
potato

eggplant (optional)
olive oil
fresh basil, chopped
fresh garlic, minced or garlic
  powder
salt and pepper, to taste
Parmesan cheese

Slice the vegetables very thinly and place them in a large baking pan slightly overlapped. Brush the vegetables with olive oil (hot pepper seasoned oil may be used). Sprinkle fresh chopped basil over everything. Add some fresh garlic or garlic powder, salt and pepper. Bake at 350 degrees uncovered for 45 minutes. Top the vegetables with 1 tablespoon of Parmesan cheese.

Christine Popper
Four Springs Farm
Royalton, Vermont

65106-05

# JANET SCOTT'S CHINESE CUCUMBER SALAD

2-3 cucumbers, thinly sliced
2 bunching onions, thinly sliced
1 red bell pepper, seeded and
   thinly sliced (optional)

salt, to taste
sugar, to taste

Sprinkle sliced cucumbers with salt and sugar, let them sit in a colander for 15 to 30 minutes. Rinse well and pat dry.

## Dressing

1 T. sesame oil
1 tsp. minced fresh ginger
1 small garlic clove, minced
2 T. seasoned rice vinegar or
   white wine vinegar
1 T. soy sauce

½ tsp. sugar
2 T. chopped peanuts, salted
   and roasted
¼ to ½ teaspoon hot chili
   pepper, seeded and minced

Mix together in a medium bowl until sugar dissolves. Add cucumbers, onion, red bell pepper and toss until coated with dressing. Chill and serve.

**Recipe Note:** Use this versatile dressing for other salads too!

Amy Nichols, Clemson University
Calhoun Field Laboratory Student Organic Farm
Clemson, South Carolina

# WINTER BEAUTY SALAD

## (This salad can be eaten any time of the day!)

1 large or 2 small beets, peeled and grated

6 medium carrots, grated
1-2 apples, cored and grated

OPTIONAL: dried cranberries, raisins, coconut, grated ginger, toasted sunflower seeds, sesame seeds, pecans, walnuts, orange sections

**Dressing**

3-5 T. lemon or lime juice
3-5 T. honey or fruit juice
(apple or orange are good)

Mix grated apples, beets, and carrots in a bowl. Add some of the optional ingredients or add some other favorite salad stir-ins. Add dressing. Stir and serve. Serves 4 to 6.

**Recipe Note:** This salad is a beautiful, bright, sweet and crunchy solution to the winter blues. It is a template. You can be creative with it. There are so many variations on the theme, and they all taste great! What fun! Enjoy.

Aimee Good
Charlestown Cooperative Farm
Phoenixville, Pennsylvania

65106-05

# JOHNNY LUV'S OUTRAGEOUS GRILLED PIZZA

## (Delight your guests at an outdoor gathering!)

1 c. warm water
1 package dry yeast or ¼
 ounces compressed yeast
2-½ to 3 c. unbleached all-
 purpose flour

2 T. olive oil
½ tsp. salt

Combine the water, yeast and 1-½ cups of flour in a mixing bowl. Mix well. Add the oil and salt, and remaining flour. Work dough in a mixer or by hand until it holds its shape. (You may need to adjust flour a bit, so add the last half gradually.) Knead the dough on a floured surface until it is smooth and elastic. Transfer the dough to a large, lightly oiled bowl. Cover and place in a warm area until it has doubled in size, about one hour. After the dough has risen, divide into hand-sized balls and place on a floured surface. Cover and let sit for 15 minutes. When ready, roll into smaller-sized pizzas that will fit two at a time, side by side on your grill surface.

### Pizza Toppings

arugula: fresh, lightly steamed or made into a pesto with garlic and olive oil
fresh garlic or scapes, chopped
cheese: mozzarella, Romano or Parmesan, shredded or grated
heirloom tomatoes: Brandywine or Cherokee Purple
basil or fresh pesto

onions: grilled, sautéed or caramelized: Purplette, Red Long of Tropea or Cioppolini
spinach, lightly steamed
eggplant: grilled or sautéed
mesculin greens
potatoes: thinly sliced and baked (added on a pizza with arugula and rosemary)

Roll out one pizza dough on a lightly floured surface. Place dough on the grill. It takes about 1 to 3 minutes for the dough to cook (adjust temperature accordingly). While the first dough is cooking, quickly roll out a second dough and place it on the other side of the grill. This speeds up the process by working two pizzas at a time. When the first
(continued)

dough has become lightly crisped and golden brown on the bottom, flip it over and cover it liberally with the garlic, olive oil, and then add whatever ingredients you wish. By the time the ingredients are placed on the first pizza, the second one should be ready to flip. Keep an eye on the bottom of the dough. Take off the grill when bottom side of the pizza is browned.

**Recipe Note:** The sky's the limit, so be creative. I prefer white pizzas without marinara sauce. I like to adjust the toppings according to what is coming out of the field at that particular time. Half the fun is letting your guests have a hand at making his or her own creations! -John

John Steward
Maple Rock Farm
Orcas Island, Washington

# CABBAGE AND BEET MEDLEY
## (An interesting combination!)

leeks, rinsed well and chopped
beets, cleaned, peeled, and cut
  into 1 inch pieces
2 garlic cloves, minced
½ head cabbage, thinly sliced

⅛ tsp. allspice
dash of cinnamon
3 T. white wine or water
1 handful of raisins

Cut leeks and beets (set aside the greens) in 1 inch pieces. Add leeks, beets and garlic and caramelize over medium heat (about 30 minutes). While the other vegetables are cooking, thinly slice half a head of cabbage. Once the other vegetables are done, add the cabbage, allspice and cinnamon. Add a few tablespoons of wine or water; cover and cook for an additional 15 to 20 minutes, checking cabbage's doneness. Add raisins before removing from the stove.

Teresa Wolcott
Many Hands Organic Farm
Barre, Massachusetts

65106-05

# SUMMERTIME PASTA

2-3 T. olive oil
2 garlic cloves, minced
1 medium onion, chopped
1/4 c. chopped celery
3-4 banana peppers, seeded
and sliced in thin strips
3 c. assorted summer squash
(patty pan, zucchini, and
crookneck) cut into bite sized
pieces

2 T. chopped fresh parsley
3 T. chopped fresh basil
salt and pepper, to taste
5-6 c. chopped fresh tomatoes
1 lb. whole-wheat angel hair
pasta or spaghetti
1/2 c. freshly grated Parmesan
cheese

In olive oil sauté the garlic, onion and celery. When soft, add the banana peppers and cook 3 to 4 minutes. Add the summer squash, parsley and basil and cook 10 minutes. Add salt and pepper to taste. Remove from heat. Chop the tomatoes and place in a large bowl. Add the sautéed vegetables and stir. Let set at room temperature while the pasta is cooking. When the pasta is ready, drain and rinse with cold water. Drain again and place in a large bowl. Add olive oil and fresh grated Parmesan cheese and toss lightly. Serve the pasta and then the tomato sauce at room temperature. Also pass Parmesan cheese for individual tastes.

Diane Weiland
Henry A. Wallace Country Life Center
Orient, Iowa

# SUMMER VEGGIE PIE
## (Quick, easy, fresh and delicious!)

2 c. chopped tomatoes (no
  need to peel)
2 c. other chopped veggies -
  onions, summer squash,
  peppers, corn, beans or any
  other fresh vegetables

fresh herbs
1 box cornbread mix, mixed
  according to box directions

Chop all vegetables into an ovenproof casserole dish. Bake at 400 degrees for 20 minutes or microwave for 8 minutes until vegetables are partially cooked. Remove from oven and top with the cornbread mix, mixed according to package instructions. Bake for an additional 20 minutes until cornbread is nicely browned. Serves 4 to 6.

**Recipe Note:** One of our previous CSA members came up with this and cooked it often in his solar oven! I love the fact you can use anything that is fresh from the field! -Robbins

Robbins Hail
Bear Creek Farms
Osceola, Missouri

65106-05

# SQUASH AND GREEN TOMATO CASSEROLE

## (This is an easy potluck casserole!)

4 large squash (yellow or zucchini), sliced
2 large green tomatoes, sliced
1 small onion, chopped

salt and pepper, to taste
½ c. sharp cheddar cheese
10 salted crackers, crushed
butter

Cook squash, tomatoes and onions in 2 cups of water. Add salt and pepper to taste. Cook until tender. Drain. In a 9 x 13 pan, place in layers: squash mixture, cheese, squash mixture, then top with cheese. Sprinkle cracker crumbs on top and dot with butter. Bake at 400 degrees until brown.

**Recipe Note:** Our CSA farm is different in that we are part of the South Plains Food Bank in Lubbock, TX. We use our farm as a job skills and life skills training ground for teens in our GRUB - Growing Recruits for Urban Business program. This recipe is a favorite at the farm. - Jennifer

Jennifer Smith
South Plains Food Bank
Lubbock, Texas

# Quinoa Salad

1 c. quinoa
1-1/2 c. water
2 tomatoes, finely chopped
6 scallions, finely sliced

1 c. finely chopped parsley and/
  or cilantro
1/4 can black olives

### Dressing

1/4 c. lemon or lime juice
2 T. olive oil
freshly ground black pepper, to
  taste

1/2 tsp. sweet marjoram
1/4 tsp. ground cumin

Whisk dressing ingredients together. Put quinoa in pan, rinse until water runs clear. Add 1-1/2 cups of water, bring to boil, reduce heat. Cook, uncovered for 15 to 20 minutes over low heat. Allow to cool for 10 minutes; add remaining ingredients. Toss with dressing to mix. May be served hot, at room temperature, or cold.

Tom McCracken
Green Earth Farm
Saguache, Colorado

*"When we see land as a community to which we belong, we may begin to use it with love and respect."*

*Aldo Leopold*

65106-05

# STRING BEAN, SUMMER SQUASH AND PEPPER STIR FRY

**(For a complete meal, serve over rice or pasta!)**

2 tsp. ground cumin
1 T. paprika
1 tsp. ground ginger
1 T. sugar
pinch of cayenne pepper
salt and pepper, to taste
4 T. oil
2-4 garlic cloves, crushed
1 onion, sliced

1 red bell pepper, sliced
1 yellow bell pepper, sliced
1 large zucchini, sliced
1 large yellow squash, sliced or
   several sunburst squash,
   sliced
6 oz. fresh green beans
1 T. lime juice
1 T. honey

Mix together the cumin, paprika, ginger, sugar, cayenne pepper, salt and pepper. Heat the oil in a large frying pan or wok. Cook the garlic and onions for a few minutes. Add the remaining vegetables and seasoning. Cook over medium heat until the vegetables begin to soften (6 to 8 minutes). Add the lime juice and honey. Heat for 3 more minutes and serve.

Friends of Old Maids Farm
Glastonbury, Connecticut

# THE DISAPPEARING SALAD

## (Created especially for substitutions!)

4 medium carrots, sliced thinly
1 large apple, sliced thinly
1 large pear, sliced thinly
1 small jicama, cut into small chunks
1 pineapple, cut into small chunks

1 bunch baby spinach
1-½ c. golden raisins
1 c. nuts or seeds, toasted
½ small red onion, finely minced
10-12 basil leaves, shredded

Combine all fruits and vegetables in a bowl. Mix gently.

## Salad Dressing

2 limes
4 T. walnut, peanut or sesame oil
2 T. honey

2 tsp. cracked white pepper
¼ tsp. ground cardamom
minced basil, to taste
freshly grated ginger, to taste

In a small saucepan, warm oil. Zest limes, then cut limes in half and squeeze juice into pan. Add lime zest and honey. Heat until honey melts (don't boil). Add pepper, cardamom, basil and ginger. Heat for a little longer, then remove. Cool for just a few minutes, then pour over salad and toss.

**Recipe Note:** A jicama has thin, brown skin and crisp juicy flesh. Peel the papery skin with a paring knife; store extra cut pieces of jicama in a container of cold water.

Renee (Ray) Bertsch
Tantre Farm
Chelsea, Michigan

65106-05

# WINTER SQUASH TAMALES
(These freeze well!)

The Masa (delicious corn
  dough)

4 c. cooked hominy
2-1/2 c. coconut oil
2 T. salt

3 T. baking powder
3 c. stock, (corncob, vegetable
  or chicken stock)

Bring stock to boil. Whip the coconut oil until fluffy and separated.
Mix the masa: hominy, salt, and baking powder. Whip the masa/hominy
mixture into the coconut oil, then add the stock, continuing to mix.
Cover with a damp cloth.

The Tamales Filling

4 c. cooked and mashed winter
  squash
2 c. chopped pepitas (pumpkin
  seeds), toasted
2 c. chopped roasted red
  peppers, drained

hot peppers (smoked chipotle
  peppers work great), chopped
  and salted, to taste

Combine all ingredients. Pumpkin seeds and roasted peppers can be
chopped in food processor, but mash the squash to avoid a wet purée.

Filling the Tamales

3-4 packages of corn husks,
  soaked in warm water for
  several hours or overnight

Take a large corn husk and put a handful of masa in the center. Make
an indentation with a spoon and add the filling. Pull the sides of the
corn husk toward each other and the tamale will form. Fold the other
two ends and tie either with a string or with the length of a corn husk
(or possibly two corn husks tied together). Steam in a steamer lined
with corn husks in batches for 45 minutes. Makes about 90.

(continued)

**Recipe Note:** A labor intensive process, but definitely worth it! Put on your favorite music and roll up your sleeves while filling the tamales! -Lisa

Lisa Jessup
Common Ground Farm
Beacon, New York

# CRUSTLESS GARDEN QUICHE

## (Serve at an August brunch when veggies are ripe!)

3 c. grated zucchini
1/2 c. chopped onion
3 tomatoes, seeded and
chopped
1 c. broccoli florets
1/2 c. sliced mushrooms
1 c. flour
2 tsp. baking powder
1/2 tsp. salt
1/4 tsp. pepper
2 tsp. dried parsley or 2
tablespoons of fresh parsley

1/2 tsp. rosemary
1/2 tsp. garlic powder or 1 clove
garlic, crushed
1/2 tsp. dried oregano or 1-1/2
teaspoons of fresh oregano
1/2 tsp. dried basil or 1-1/2
teaspoons of fresh basil
10 eggs
3/4 c. grated Parmesan cheese
4 T. butter, melted
1-1/2 c. grated cheddar cheese

Combine vegetables and set aside. Combine flour, baking powder, seasonings and herbs, and set aside. Beat eggs with a whisk in a large bowl. Add Parmesan cheese and melted butter and stir well to combine. Add flour mixture and stir well. Add vegetables and stir to combine. Place in a buttered 9 x 13 glass pan. Top with cheddar cheese. Bake at 350 degrees for 50 minutes to 1 hour. Let stand 15 minutes before serving.

Theresa Williams
Pond House Farm CSA
Manton, Michigan

65106-05

# HOG'S BACK FARM'S MAPLE PURÉE
## (This tastes like Autumn but with a twist!)

4 T. butter
1 onion, chopped
3 carrots, peeled (or well-scrubbed), thinly sliced
1 butternut squash (about 3-½ lbs.) peeled, seeded and cut into ½-inch pieces

1 c. fresh orange juice
3 T. pure maple syrup

Melt 2 tablespoons of butter in a large pot over medium heat. Add onion and sauté until just tender, 8 minutes. Stir in 1 tablespoon of butter. Add squash and sauté until squash begins to soften, 8 minutes. Pour orange juice over vegetables. Cover and simmer until vegetables are soft, 25 minutes. Uncover and simmer until all liquid evaporates, 5 minutes. Stir in maple syrup, cool slightly. Working in batches, purée mixture in food processor until smooth. Season to taste with salt and pepper. Transfer to serving bowl.

**Recipe Note:** This dish can be made two days ahead. Cover and refrigerate. Stir over medium heat to re-warm.

David Van Eeckhout
Hog's Back Farm
Arkansaw, Wisconsin

# ROSEMARY-GRILLED VEGETABLES

## (Fresh rosemary was made for grilled veggies!)

1 medium sweet onion, outer
peel removed, halved
2 medium red bell peppers,
stemmed, halved, and seeded
1 medium zucchini cut
lengthwise into ½ inch thick
slices
1 T. extra-virgin olive oil
1 tsp. sea salt

½ tsp. coarsely ground black
pepper
2 T. finely chopped fresh
rosemary leaves
1 medium head red oak leaf
lettuce, leaves separated and
rinsed well
20 pitted and sliced Kalamata
olives

Preheat barbeque grill. Place onion, pepper and zucchini on grill. Brush with olive oil and sprinkle with salt, pepper and rosemary. Grill, turning once or twice, until browned on both sides and tender, about 15 minutes. Set aside to cool completely. (Vegetables may also be roasted in oven at 450 degrees for 20 minutes or until tender.)

### Citrus Dressing

¼ c. grapefruit juice
2 T. extra virgin olive oil
2 garlic cloves, crushed

½ tsp. sea salt
½ tsp. black pepper

Combine grapefruit juice, olive oil, garlic, salt and black pepper in a small mixing bowl and blend well. Place lettuce on plate. Top with vegetables. Sprinkle with olives. Drizzle dressing over vegetables just before serving.

Karen Vollmecke
Vollmecke Orchards CSA
West Brandywine, Pennsylvania

65106-05

# GREEK-STYLE ONE-DISH MEAL
## (Make this for a friend to say "thank you!")

| | |
|---|---|
| 1 lb. ground beef | 2 tomatoes, diced |
| 1 onion, diced | 2 c. cut green beans |
| 1 garlic clove, minced | 2 T. tomato paste |
| 12 c. beef broth | 2 tsp. oregano |
| 1-1/2 c. whole-wheat penne | 1/2 tsp. ground cinnamon |
|   pasta, uncooked | 1 c. feta cheese |

In a large saucepan, brown beef with onion and garlic. Add broth and bring to a boil. Add pasta. Return to a boil. Stir in all ingredients except feta cheese. Return to a boil. Add 1/2 cup of feta cheese. Simmer until sauce thickens, about 7 to 10 minutes. Sprinkle with remaining cheese.

Jeanine Jenks Farley
Waltham Fields Community Farm
Waltham, Massachusetts

# COMMON GROUND FARM'S RATATOUILLE

## (Fresh herbs intensify the flavor.)

3 T. extra virgin olive oil
2 c. chopped onions
4 garlic cloves, minced
2 lbs. eggplant, unpeeled and cubed
2 medium zucchini or summer squash, cubed
2 bell peppers, any color, chopped

3 lbs. ripe tomatoes, chopped
3 fresh thyme sprigs
1 fresh rosemary sprig
½ c. chopped fresh basil
½ c. chopped fresh parsley
salt and freshly ground black pepper, to taste

Heat oil in a large pot over medium heat. Add onions and sauté until translucent about 10 minutes. Add garlic and eggplant and sauté 5 minutes. Add zucchini and peppers and sauté 5 minutes. Mix in tomatoes, thyme, rosemary, salt and black pepper. Reduce heat to low. Cover and cook until vegetables are very tender, stirring occasionally, for about an hour. Adjust seasonings and add basil and parsley. Serve hot, warm or cold. Serves 4 to 6.

**Recipe Note:** This is a classic French stew, designed for what you have on hand. Measurements are approximate and ingredients can change with the harvest.

Lee Ann Pomplas
Common Ground Farm
Beacon, New York

65106-05

# GREEN LENTIL SALAD

## (Great for energy! Packed with protein and fiber!)

½ c. green lentils
2 c. water
1 strip of kombu, seaweed
1 red pepper, chopped
1 tomato, chopped
5 mushrooms, sliced
2 garlic cloves, sliced

½ avocado, chopped
4 shallots
2 tsp. balsamic vinegar
2 tsp. olive oil
1 T. fresh rosemary
black pepper and salt, to taste

Soak lentils overnight and drain water. Bring 2 cups of water, kombu and lentils to a boil. Remove kombu once boiled and reduce heat and simmer for 20 minutes. Season with salt. Simmer until tender. Drain lentils and rinse in water. In a dry fry pan, roast garlic until toasted and fragrant. Mix all ingredients together and serve with garlic as a topping.

Deborah Hildebrandt
Be Wise Ranch CSA
San Diego, California

# CORN FRITTERS
## (Use leftover corn on the cob!)

3 c. cooked corn (cut off the cob)
2 eggs, separated, whites beaten until soft peaks form

2 T. flour
¼ tsp. salt
black pepper, to taste
oil/butter

Mix corn, egg yolks, flour, salt and pepper. If mixture is very dry add 1 to 2 tablespoons of milk or sour cream. Fold in beaten egg whites. Fry pancakes in oil or oil/butter mixture at medium to med/high heat. These are great hot with salt or can be served with maple syrup. Yields: 12 to 15 three inch fritters.

**Recipe Note:** They also freeze well, and then they can be microwaved. Corn fritters are great for breakfast, but I like them as a side with a good garden rich dinner. -Patty

Patty Aune
H & H Organic Farms
Raleigh, North Carolina

*"In my opinion, Community Supported Agriculture is nothing short of a revolution in the way we grow, distribute and eat our food."*
Jim Leap, UC Santa Cruz Farm, Farm Manager

65106-05

# INVERBROOK CHICKEN AND SUMMER VEGETABLE STEW

## (serve with potatoes, rice, or couscous)

1 eggplant, peeled and cut into 1-inch pieces
3 tsp. olive oil
1 tsp. salt
1 T. herbs de Provence
1 chicken (3-4 lbs) cut into at least quarters
2 onions, chopped
2 garlic cloves, diced

3 peppers (red, orange and/or green) cut into strips or 1 inch pieces
1 zucchini cut into 1 inch cubes
4 tomatoes, quartered
1 T. lemon juice
fresh black pepper and additional herbs, to taste

Salt eggplant cubes, let them sit for about 15 minutes then drain and rinse. Heat oil in a large Dutch oven over medium heat. Brown chicken with salt and herbs de Provence (about 5 minutes for each batch of chicken pieces). Remove chicken and set aside. Add onion and garlic to Dutch oven. Sauté until onion is tender, about 2 minutes. Add peppers and cook for 2 minutes stirring constantly. Add eggplant, zucchini, tomatoes, lemon juice and other herbs or spices of your choice. Mix well. Return chicken to Dutch oven with remaining vegetables. Surround chicken with vegetables. Simmer uncovered for 30 minutes (until chicken is cooked and vegetables are tender). Serve chicken and vegetables over potatoes, rice, or couscous.

Claire Murray
Inverbrook Farm CSA
West Grove, Pennsylvania

# VEGGIE PIZZA

## (Best baked on a pizza stone!)

### Dough

1 c. warm water
1 T. sugar
2-¼ tsp. active dry yeast

3 T. olive oil
1 tsp. salt
2-½ c. all-purpose flour

### Pizza Toppings

2 tomatoes, thinly sliced
1 red pepper, sliced
1 sweet onion, sliced
1 T. minced garlic
seasonings such as basil,
  oregano, rosemary, thyme,
  cracked black pepper

2 c. shredded cheese, such as
  mozzarella or Parmesan

Stir water, sugar and yeast together until dissolved. Add the olive oil and the salt. Stir in the flour until well blended. Let dough rest for 10 minutes. Pat dough into greased pan or onto a pizza stone using fingers dipped in olive oil. If desired, sprinkle oregano, rosemary, thyme or other seasonings on crust. Thinly slice 2 tomatoes, an onion, and a pepper, etc. and place on top. Drizzle olive oil over the toppings and bake as directed. (Add your favorite cheese: Parmesan, mozzarella, feta, etc. during the last 5 minutes of cooking). Add your favorite pizza toppings and bake in a preheated 425 degree oven for 15 to 20 minutes. During the last 5 minutes place under a broiler until the top gets golden brown.

Dave Chirico & Matt Ferut
Two Guys Farm
Reynoldsville, Pennsylvania

65106-05

# GOOD SPANISH RICE

1 lb. bacon (optional)
2 onions
2 bell peppers, one red, one green
1 (28 oz.) can of whole tomatoes or use the equivalent of fresh tomatoes
1 (15 oz.) can of tomato sauce
2 tsp. salt
4 tsp. sugar
1 (7 oz.) can of diced green chilies
2 (8 oz.) cans of sliced water chestnuts
3 (2.25 oz.) cans of sliced olives (green, black or a combination)
2-3/4 c. long grain rice
3/4 lb. cheddar cheese
2 avocados, sliced
4 green onions

In a large 3-1/2 quart pot, fry bacon until crisp, drain and save 2 tablespoons of oil for onions and peppers. Crumble bacon and set aside as a topping. Fry onions in bacon fat until browned. Cross section each bell pepper and chop one half of each, reserving the other half of each to slice into rings for topping. Add diced pepper to onions, cook until soft. Drain liquid from tomatoes into measuring cup. Add enough water to make 3-1/2 cups of liquid. Cut tomatoes into bite-sized pieces. Add tomatoes, liquid, tomato sauce, salt and sugar to peppers and onions. Bring to a boil. Immediately remove and stir in chilies, water chestnuts, olives and rice. Pour into a large 3 quart casserole dish and cover. Bake at 350 degrees for 75 minutes. Fluff rice, sprinkle with cheese and return to oven uncovered for 5 minutes. Remove and garnish with avocado, pepper, green onion and bacon.

**Recipe Note:** For a lower fat version of this recipe, omit the bacon and use 2 tablespoons of olive oil instead. It still tastes great!

Deborah Hildebrandt
Be Wise Ranch CSA
San Diego, California

# EGGPLANT-SPINACH MANICOTTI

## Sauce

2 T. olive oil
2 medium onions
2 large carrots, chopped
1/2 c. red wine
5 large garlic cloves, crushed
10 Roma or 5 beefsteak
tomatoes

1 c. vegetable broth
1 c. chopped fresh basil
1 tsp. fresh thyme and
marjoram
1 tsp. salt, if desired
dash of black pepper

Place olive oil in pan at medium heat. Add onions and carrots; sauté until tender. Add wine and garlic and cook 5 more minutes. Add the peeled and chopped tomatoes, vegetable stock, herbs, salt and pepper. Bring to a slow simmer; continue simmering for 30 minutes.

## Filling

1 lb. ricotta cheese
5 oz. Asiago or Romano Cheese
2 c. shredded spinach

1/2 tsp. nutmeg
1/4 tsp. cayenne pepper
2 medium eggs

Pour off any liquid from ricotta. In a large mixing bowl add ricotta, Asiago, spinach, nutmeg, cayenne and eggs. Mix.

## Shells

3 medium eggplants, cut
lengthwise into 1/3 inch thick
slices

1/4 c. olive oil
1/2 c. freshly grated Parmesan
cheese

Oil 2 to 3 baking sheets. Arrange olive oil brushed eggplant slices on sheet. Bake at 350 degrees for 15 to 20 minutes or until tender. Let eggplant pieces cool on baking sheets.

Spread half of the sauce over the bottom of a large glass baking dish (13 x 9 x 2). Once the eggplant is cooled, place a slice on a working surface and drop 1/4 cup of filling or less on the narrow end of the eggplant. Roll up the eggplant slices with the filling inside. Arrange the

(continued)

eggplant shells in a single layer on top of the sauce. Once you have placed all of the shells in the pan, pour the remaining sauce over the top. Bake at 350 degrees for approximately 30 minutes. Ten minutes before the dish is finished baking, top with Parmesan cheese.

Jon Behling
Back To Our Roots Farm
Chippewa Falls, Wisconsin

# FLAMING SOUP
## (Fresh for a sunny day!)

2 beets
10 carrots
10 celery stalks
4-6 tomatoes
2 handfuls of almonds

1 T. fresh thyme and basil
juice of one lemon
chives
yogurt

Juice all vegetables except tomatoes. Chop tomatoes and almonds or pulse in a food processor. Combine and serve topped with yogurt and chives.

**Recipe Note:** Great for cleansing your system and tastes good too! Serve cold on a hot summer day! -Deborah

Deborah Hildebrandt
Be Wise Ranch CSA
San Diego, California

# ROASTED CORN RELISH
## (Compliments of Pete Fenczik)

4 ears of corn
1 T. chopped parsley or basil
4 T. finely chopped red onion
4 T. finely chopped roasted red
    pepper
1/4 c. lime juice

1/4 c. olive oil
16 cherry tomatoes, cut into
    halves
salt and pepper, to taste
1/2 tsp. cumin seeds, toasted &
    ground (or use cumin powder)

Shuck the corn and remove the silk. Broil or grill the corn until slightly browned, turn frequently to avoid burning. Cut the kernels from the cob into a mixing bowl. Add remaining ingredients to the kernels and let stand one hour. Taste and adjust seasoning. Serve or refrigerate.

Stephen & Gloria Decater
Live Power Community Farm
Covelo, California

**Recipe Favorites**

65106-05

# BROCCOLI, CAULIFLOWER, & CABBAGE

# BROCCOLI, CAULIFLOWER & CABBAGE

## COLESLAW
### (A classic!)

red and green cabbage, grated
1 onion, chopped
mayonnaise

sugar
salt
lemon juice

In a food processor, grate a mixture of red and green cabbage along with 1 onion. Mix with enough mayonnaise to moisten. Add sugar, salt, and lemon juice to taste.

**Recipe Note:** Grate the cabbage and go from there, tasting until it seems right!

Anne Morgan
Lakes & Valley CSA/Midheaven Farms
Park Rapids, Minnesota

# CHINESE COLESLAW

1/2 lb. shredded cabbage, or
   more as desired
1 pkg. chicken ramen noodles,
   crushed (use seasoning
   later)

1/4 lb. slivered almonds,
   toasted
3 T. sesame seeds, toasted
4 green onions, sliced

To toast almonds and seeds, put on cookie sheet in oven for a few minutes or toast on stove in a skillet on medium heat and watch, stirring often; let them cool before using in slaw. In a large bowl, combine cabbage and green onions.

## Dressing

1/4 c. cider vinegar
1/8 c. sugar
1/2 c. vegetable oil
seasoning pack from the
   Raman noodles

2 tsp. salt
1 tsp. pepper

Mix dressing together and pour over cabbage and green onions. Add crushed noodles, toasted almonds and sesame seeds just before serving.

Donna Handley-Lynch
Michaela Farm
Oldenburg, Indiana

65106-05

# CHINESE CABBAGE WITH MISO GRAVY

1 large package of ramen
  noodles
1 med. Chinese cabbage,
  chopped
sesame oil

1-1/2 c. chopped toasted
  almonds
miso
tamari
chili paste (optional)

Make the ramen noodles according to the package directions. Sauté the cabbage in sesame oil until just wilted, but still has some crunch, toss in almonds and remove from heat. Make a 'miso gravy' by adding just enough water to the miso to make a thick sauce, add tamari to taste. Add sauce to cabbage mixture to taste (extra can always be served on the side). Drain noodles and toss with cabbage and serve. Chili paste can be served on the side for those who like more heat.

Desiree Robertson-DuBois
Crabapple Farm
Chesterfield, Massachusetts

# FRESH JAYNE'S COLESLAW

1/2 head cabbage (any color)
  chopped into 1/2 inch pieces
  (about 2 1/2 cups)
1/2 c. mayonnaise

2 T. honey
1 T. stone ground mustard
1 carrot, shredded
2 T. fresh chopped parsley

Mix everything together in one bowl. Chill and serve. "Easy Peasy!"

**Recipe Note:** Many of our CSA members were unaccustomed to using cabbage. This is an easy, fresh tasting coleslaw that people love. Even if you think you don't like cabbage, give this a try! -Janye and Ryan

Jayne and Ryan Senecal
Golden Root CSA at Earth Care Farm
Charlestown, Rhode Island

# MAPLE VIEW COLESLAW
## (An old family recipe)

¼ c. mustard
⅓ c. mayonnaise
¼ c. oil

¼ c. cider vinegar
½ cabbage, shredded
salt and pepper, to taste

Put the first 4 ingredients in a small bowl and combine with a whisk. This is now the dressing for the shredded cabbage. Pour dressing over cabbage and season with salt and pepper to taste.

Carole Gauger
Maple View Farm
Harwinton, Connecticut


# TANGY FRUIT SLAW
## (Great for a gathering!)

½ c. mayonnaise
¼ c. plain yogurt
3 T. Dijon mustard
2 T. honey
1 tsp. celery seed

3 c. shredded cabbage
2 apples
1 c. raisins
1 c. sunflower seeds

Stir together mayonnaise, yogurt, mustard, honey and celery seed. Shred cabbage, add dressing and toss. Dice unpeeled apples and add to cabbage mixture with raisins and sunflower seeds. Stir well to mix, cover, and chill. Serves 6.

Harriet Kattenburg
Seedtime & Harvest
Hull, Iowa


*"No occupation is so delightful to me as the culture of the earth, and no culture comparable to that of the garden. But though an old man, I am but a young gardener."*

*Thomas Jefferson*

65106-05

# CABBAGE SALAD

½ c. sugar
1 tsp. dry mustard
1 c. olive oil or the oil of your choice
1 tsp. salt
2 tsp. grated onion

½ c. apple cider vinegar
1 tsp. celery seed
½ medium head of cabbage
3 medium carrots (orange, yellow, and red)

Shake together all ingredients except carrots and cabbage in a glass pint jar. Shred cabbage and carrots. Add enough dressing to moisten the vegetables and serve. The extra dressing will keep in the refrigerator for up to six weeks.

Mary Pat Klawitter
Klawitter CSA
Euclid, Minnesota

# BRAISED CABBAGE WITH APPLES

2 T. olive or vegetable oil
1 c. chopped onion
1 head of cabbage, about 1-½ lbs., cored and thinly sliced
2 apples, granny smith or other firm, tart variety
½ c. golden raisins

⅓ c. dry red wine
⅓ c. red wine vinegar
1-½ T. dark brown sugar
1-½ tsp. chopped fresh thyme
¼ tsp. freshly ground pepper
¼ tsp. salt

Remove core from apple and cut into ¾ to 1 inch dice. Heat oil in Dutch oven or large, deep frying pan over medium-low heat. Add onions and sauté until soft, about 10 minutes. Add the remaining ingredients. Increase heat to medium and cover the pan. Cook, stirring occasionally, for one hour. Cabbage should be soft but not mushy. If still crisp, continue to cook, checking every 10 minutes or so. Taste and add more salt and pepper, if desired. Serves 4.

Susie Wood
Provident Farm
Bivalve, Maryland

# CABBAGE PIE
## (This pie is even great eaten cold the next day!)

| | |
|---|---|
| 1 large cabbage | salt and pepper |
| $1/2$-1 lb. fresh mushrooms | dash of tamari soy sauce |
| 1 (8-oz.) pkg. cream cheese | 2 unbaked pie crusts |

Cut up the cabbage and lightly steam. Sauté the mushrooms, just enough to get some of the moisture off. Place $1/4$ inch wedges of cream cheese on the bottom of one (unbaked) pie crust. Place about $1/2$ inch layer of cabbage on top of cream cheese. Next, put a similar layer of mushrooms. Sprinkle with salt, pepper, and a dash of tamari. Continue to alternate in this manner until your pie crust is very full (can be filled above the top). Place the second pie crust on top and seal the edges. Cut vent holes in the top crust and bake at 350 degrees for about 50 minutes or until the crust is brown and flaky.

Christa Backson-Crane
Community Environmental Council Urban Farm
Santa Barbara, California

65106-05

# HAM AND CABBAGE
## (An easy winter, one pot meal!)

1 smoked daisy roll ham (pork
   shoulder butt) (approx 2 lbs)
2 bay leaves
1 large onion, peeled and
   quartered
1 lb. carrots, peeled

1 large cabbage
6 large potatoes, peeled
½ tsp. freshly ground pepper
golden mustard of your choice
3 T. butter

Place the ham into a stockpot (at least 8 quarts). Cover the ham with water. Add bay leaves, onion and one carrot. Bring to a boil, reduce heat to a simmer. Simmer covered for 1-½ hours. Meanwhile, prepare the vegetables. Quarter the cabbage, removing the core, cut each quarter into chunks. Cut the potatoes and carrots into 2 inch chunks. Remove ham and bay leaves from the pot. Wrap ham in foil to keep warm. Add the vegetables and black pepper. Simmer covered until the vegetables are tender. Serve vegetables in a large soup bowl. Put a pat of butter on top of the vegetables. Slice ham and serve with golden mustard.

**Recipe Note:** This one pot dish is an old dinner favorite that Mom always made. The juices thicken from the starch in the potatoes and come alive with the flavor of the ham. A loaf of fresh crusty bread such as rye is a must to mop up your bowl! Substitute corned beef instead of ham for a flavorful St. Patrick's Day dinner! -Julie

Julie Sochacki

# ROBIN'S CABBAGE-TOMATO SIDE DISH
(Robin improvised and made this delicious dish.)

½ c. water
2 c. grated cabbage
1 c. sweet onion

4 medium tomatoes, cubed
1 tsp. celery seed
salt and pepper, to taste

In a large frying pan, cook cabbage and onion in water until tender. Add tomatoes until warm. Turn off heat and add celery seed and salt and pepper to taste. Serve immediately.

Tim and Robin Leonard
Garden Patch Farm
Pinckney, Michigan


# SWEET-AND-SOUR ROTKRAUT

2 T. olive oil
4 medium apples, peeled and
   sliced
½ red onion, chopped
1 red cabbage, finely shredded
1 c. red wine

4 whole cloves
⅓ c. brown sugar
2 bay leaves
2 T. lemon juice
½ c. red wine vinegar
salt and pepper to taste

Sauté the apples and onions in olive oil for two minutes on medium-low heat. Add the cabbage, red wine, cloves, sugar, and bay leaves and bring to simmer. Cover, reduce heat, and cook for 1 hour. Add the lemon juice, vinegar, and salt and pepper. (Melt a pat of butter into it just before serving.) Serves 6.

Tom McElderry
Eatwell Farm
Dixon, California

65106-05

# INDONESIAN BAMI

5 T. olive or vegetable oil,
   divided
2 garlic cloves, minced
1/2 tsp. crushed red pepper
1 lb. flank steak, cut across the
   grain in strips
1/2 lb. medium raw shrimp, cut
   in half lengthwise

2 green onions, 1/2 inch slices
2 c. shredded cabbage (slice
   thinly with knife)
1 c. each leeks and celery, 1/4
   inch slices
8 oz. vermicelli, broken in half
   and cooked "al dente"
1/4 c. soy sauce

Place a wok or large fry pan over high heat. When hot, add 2 tablespoons of oil, garlic, and pepper. Stir once. Add steak and stir-fry for 1 minute; add shrimp and stir-fry until shrimp are opaque and steak is browned but pink inside (about 30 seconds). Remove from pan. Pour 2 more tablespoons of oil into the pan. Add onions, cabbage, leeks, and celery. Stir-fry until tender crisp (about 2 minutes). Add vermicelli, 1 tablespoon oil, and soy sauce. Stir-fry 1 minute. Return steak and shrimp to the pan and continue stir-frying until liquid is absorbed. Do not overcook the veggies; they should be tender crisp. Optional: the steak and shrimp can be replaced with salmon cut in 1 inch chunks.

Leigh Fosberry
Pitcher Mountain CSA
Stoddard, New Hampshire

# Romanesco dip

6 oz. chopped Parmesan or
   Romano cheese
2 bunches of parsley or
   cilantro

6 cloves of garlic
olive oil

In a processor or blender, grate cheese, then add parsley (or cilantro), garlic, and just enough olive oil to allow the processor to blend. Continue to blend until smooth.

**Recipe Note:** I serve the romanesco as part (or as all) of a raw vegetable platter with this simple-minded dip (You have to love garlic for this!). Guests can ooo and ahh over the romanesco, then slice off a piece and dip! -Karen

Karen Rosenburg
Eatwell Farm
Dixon, California

# Marlene's romanesco

1 large head of romanesco
3 large garlic cloves, peeled
1/4 c. olive oil
1/4 tsp. red pepper flakes
1/4 tsp. salt

1/2 c. chopped green olives
1/8 c. chopped parsley
zest of 1 lemon and 1
   tablespoon of lemon juice

Cut romanesco into small florets and soak in ice water for 20 minutes. Cook with garlic cloves in boiling salted water for 3 minutes. Drain and set aside. Chop garlic. Heat oil in small pot, add pepper flakes and remove pan from heat. Stir in salt, garlic, olives, parsley, lemon zest and lemon juice. Pour over romanesco and toss gently. Serves 3.

Marlene Washington
Eatwell Farm
Dixon, California

65106-05

# STEAMED BROCCOLI WITH REAL TERIYAKI SAUCE

3 tsp. sugar
½ c. sake
½ c. mirin
½ c. low-sodium soy sauce
1 tsp. cornstarch
1 lb. or more broccoli, large florets, stems peeled and sliced on a bias

roasted sesame seeds
rice, fully cooked
Optional: fully cooked meat or tofu

Bring sugar, sake, mirin, soy sauce and cornstarch to a simmer in a small saucepan. Stir until sugar dissolves and the sauce thickens, then remove from heat and cover. Steam the broccoli until bright green and just tender. It's done when fragrant. Reheat the teriyaki sauce if necessary. Mound rice on plates, arrange broccoli and meat or tofu on top, then generously pour sauce. Sprinkle with lots of roasted sesame seeds.

**Recipe Note:** Mirin is a sweet Japanese cooking wine, and it is available at any well-stocked supermarket. Also, make rice and tofu or meat and have it almost ready before steaming the broccoli, which happens quickly. -Tom

Tom McElderry
Eatwell Farm
Dixon, California

# Broccoli with Dill

1 bunch broccoli
2 T. butter or margarine
2 T. chopped fresh dill or other
   herb of your choice

1 T. fresh lemon juice

Cut broccoli into stalks or florets. Steam until tender and bright green, about 6 minutes. Heat butter, dill, and lemon juice in a small sauce pan on the stove or in a bowl in the microwave. Pour butter mixture over broccoli and serve. Serves 2 to 4.

Anna Barnes
Prarieland CSA
Champaign, Illinois

# Clouds and Trees
## (Kid-approved! Can be made the day before!)

1 head of broccoli
1 head of cauliflower
1-1/2 lbs. cooked bacon, chopped
1 red onion, sliced

1 c. of your own style and
   taste- sunflower seeds,
   raisins, black olives

### Dressing

1 c. mayonnaise
1-1/2 c. sour cream
2 T. sugar

2 T. vinegar
salt and pepper, to taste

Wash broccoli and cauliflower; trim off thick stalks using only tender florets in the salad. Toss broccoli, cauliflower, bacon, red onion and any other stir-ins in the bowl. In a separate bowl, combine mayonnaise, sour cream, sugar, and vinegar, stirring well. Pour over broccoli mixture again tossing well.

**Recipe Note:** This recipe is great to tempt children who do not want to eat their veggies! We call it "Clouds and Trees" and they love it! -Angela

Angela Thiel
St. Fairsted
Woodville, Texas

65106-05

# BROCCOLI-CAULIFLOWER FRITTERS

½ lb. fresh broccoli florets
½ lb. fresh cauliflower florets
2 c. boiling water
2 large eggs, slightly beaten
1 small onion, diced

½ c. pecans, toasted and
   chopped
½ c. self-rising flour
½ tsp. salt
vegetable oil

Cook florets in 2 cups of boiling water over medium heat, 10 to 12 minutes, or until very tender. Drain. Mash florets with a potato masher or fork in a large bowl. Stir in eggs and next 4 ingredients. Pour oil into a large skillet to a depth of ¼ inch; heat to 350 degrees. Drop broccoli mixture by tablespoonfuls into hot oil, and cook in batches, 1 to 2 minutes on each side or until lightly browned. Remove to a wire rack or on a baking sheet. Keep warm.

Jolinda Hamilton
Hamilton Farms
Clinton, Arkansas

*"I have never had so many good ideas day after day as when I worked in the garden."*

*John Erskine*

# BAKED WHOLE CAULIFLOWER
## (A King family favorite!)

1 large head cauliflower
1/2 c. seasoned bread crumbs
2 T. grated Parmesan cheese
1/4 c. margarine, melted

1/8 tsp. garlic powder
1/8 tsp. salt
1 pinch red pepper flakes
1 pinch dried oregano

Clean cauliflower, and trim off leaves and any brown spots. Place the whole head of cauliflower into a steamer basket, place the basket in a large pot, and add one inch of water. Cover, and bring to a boil over medium heat. Cook for about 20 minutes or until tender. In a medium bowl, mix together the bread crumbs, Parmesan cheese, and melted margarine. Season with garlic powder, salt, red pepper flakes, and oregano, and mix well. Place the head of the cauliflower into a baking dish, and coat with the bread crumb mixture. Bake at 375 degrees for about 10 to 15 minutes or until golden brown.

**Recipe Note:** If you thought you didn't like cauliflower, try this! It's an awesome treat for a festive table. Beautiful presentation and something out of the ordinary!

Art and Kathy King
Harvest Valley Farms
Valencia, Pennsylvania

**Recipe Favorites**

65106-05

# CARROTS, POTATOES, & OTHER ROOTS

# CARROTS, POTATOES & OTHER ROOTS

## LEMON GARLIC ROASTED BEETS
### (Lemon and garlic are a terrific combination!)

1 lb. beets, peeled and sliced $1/4$ inch thick
4 garlic cloves, thinly sliced
2 T. lemon juice

$1/4$ tsp. lemon zest
$1/2$ tsp. extra virgin olive oil
$1/4$ tsp. sugar
1 pinch each, salt and pepper

In an 8 inch square glass baking dish, toss all ingredients together. Rub a piece of parchment paper with olive oil and set oiled side down on the beets. Cover tightly with tin foil, and roast at 375 degrees for 40 minutes, shaking pan occasionally, to prevent beets from sticking to baking dish.

Kelly Saxer
Desert Roots Farm CSA
Queen Creek, Arizona

# ROASTED BEET AND TURNIP SALAD
## (An unbelievable mixture of color and flavor!)

### Roasted Beets and Turnips

15 stems fresh thyme, coarsely chopped, divided into thirds
6 stems fresh rosemary, coarsely chopped, divided into thirds
2 garlic cloves, minced
2 T. extra-virgin olive oil
10 baby beets (about 1 inch in diameter), washed, unpeeled, leaves trimmed and saved (see salad below)

4-6 turnips, washed, trimmed, peeled and cut into 6-8 wedges (about 1 pound)
salt and pepper, to taste

### Glaze

1/3 rosemary and thyme (from above)
1/4 c. canned low salt chicken broth

1 T. balsamic vinegar

### Salad

reserved beet greens (tops) from above
1 garlic clove, minced

1 T. balsamic vinegar
3 T. extra-virgin olive oil

Spray large rimmed baking sheet with nonstick spray. Mix 2/3 of thyme and rosemary, oil and garlic in small bowl. Add turnips and beets to bowl. Toss with herb mixture and transfer to baking sheet. Sprinkle with salt and pepper and roast in oven at 425 degrees, for 40 minutes, stirring once. After vegetables are roasted, mix 1/3 herbs, chicken broth and 1 tablespoon of balsamic vinegar in small bowl and pour over roasted beets and turnips on baking sheet. Return baking sheet to oven and roast until liquid evaporates and vegetables are slightly glazed about

(continued)

65106-05

5 minutes. Meanwhile prepare beet greens by tearing leaves and washing, spin in salad spinner or blot with paper towels to dry. Mix together 1 clove garlic, 1 tablespoon balsamic vinegar and 3 tablespoons olive oil in a medium bowl. Add beet greens and toss to coat. Season with salt and pepper. To serve, arrange beet greens on salad plates and top with roasted vegetables. Can be served hot or at room temperature.

Amy Nichols, Clemson University
Calhoun Field Laboratory Student Organic Farm
Clemson, South Carolina

# BEET RISOTTO WITH GREENS

2-3 T. olive oil
1 c. chopped onions
1-1/2 c. Arborio rice
1/2 c. white wine
1-1/2-2 c. shredded beets
6-7 c. warm vegetable stock (or water)

2-3 c. greens, washed and torn (beet greens go especially well, but spinach or kale can be substituted)
chopped parsley, to taste
Parmesan or Romano cheese, grated, to taste

Heat the oil in a saucepan with a lid and sauté the onion until translucent. Add the rice and sauté for about a minute. Add wine and continue to stir while it's absorbed. Add beets and stir, then add 2 cups of the stock, cover and simmer for 5 minutes, until the liquid is absorbed. Uncover and begin adding the stock a 1/2-cup at a time, stirring constantly and adding more as the liquid is absorbed. After the second addition of stock (3 cups), add the torn greens and continue to stir in. Continue to stir and add stock until at least six cups of stock have been used. Serve with parsley and cheese to taste.

Gayle Eubank
Sproutwood Farm CSA
Glen Rock, Pennsylvania

# ROASTED BEET SALAD

beets
lettuce
orange sections
goat cheese crumbles

olive oil
balsamic vinegar
orange juice
caramelized pecans

Wrap each beet in foil with a drizzle of olive oil. Bake at 350 degrees for about 45 minutes. Remove from oven, cool a bit and slip off skins. Dice beets and arrange on lettuce with orange sections and goat cheese crumbles. Dress with a vinaigrette of olive oil, balsamic vinegar and orange juice. Sprinkle with caramelized pecans.

**Recipe Note:** Make as little or as much as you want of this delicious and colorful salad!

Mary Lee Chin
Granata Farms
Denver, Colorado

65106-05

# ROASTED BEET SALAD WITH FETA
## (A Greek-inspired salad!)

6 T. extra virgin olive oil
2-1/2 T. red wine vinegar
1 T. minced garlic
salt and pepper, to taste
7 medium beets, with greens

1 c. water
2 T. capers, drained and
  chopped (optional)
3/4 c. feta

Whisk oil, vinegar and garlic in a small bowl to blend. Season dressing generously with salt and pepper. (You can also substitute any vinaigrette dressing.) Cut green tops off beets; reserve tops. Arrange beets in single layer in 13 x 9 x 2-inch baking dish; add 1 cup water. Cover; bake at 375 degrees until beets are tender when pierced with knife, about 70 minutes. Peel beets while warm. Cut beets in half and slice thinly. Transfer to large bowl. Mix in capers and 1/4 cup dressing. Season with salt and pepper. Cut stems off beet greens; discard stems. Wash greens. Transfer greens, with some water still clinging to leaves, to large pot. Stir over high heat until just wilted but still bright green, about 4 minutes. Drain greens; squeeze out excess moisture. Cool; chop coarsely. Transfer greens to medium bowl. Toss with enough dressing to coat. Season to taste with salt and pepper. Arrange beets in center of platter. Surround with greens; sprinkle with feta. Drizzle with any remaining dressing.

Solyssa Visalli
Cop Copi Farms
La Grand, Oregon

# GLAZED BEETS
## (Easy and delicious!)

chicken stock or water
salt, to taste
Red, Chiogga or Golden beets,
  sliced

2 T. butter or olive oil

In a deep skillet add about 1-1/2 inch of water or chicken stock and salt to taste. Add sliced beets. Add 2 tablespoons of butter or olive oil to the skillet. Simmer at medium-high heat until all the liquid is gone. Serve immediately.

**Recipe Note:** The liquid absorbs the flavor, the beets absorb the liquid and the butter/oil, which will float to the top and glaze the beets. Add any of these ingredients to further the flavor of the beets: fresh ginger, soy sauce, garlic, onions or fresh herbs.

Bill Brammer III
Be Wise Ranch CSA
San Diego, California


# MARINATED BEETS

1 lb. beets
1-2 tsp. crushed garlic
1-2 T. chopped fresh tarragon

2 T. olive oil
4 T. balsamic vinegar
salt and black pepper, to taste

Bake, roast or pressure steam the whole beets until tender. Let them cool until you can easily handle them, then remove the skins and chop them into small cubes or slices. Combine the rest of the ingredients in a bowl large enough to hold the beets as well, and whisk until well combined. Add the beets, toss well, and refrigerate for at least 1 hour before serving. Serve cold or at room temperature.

David Van Eeckhout
Hog's Back Farm
Arkansaw, Wisconsin

65106-05

# CARROTS & APPLE SALAD
## (A kid-approved favorite!)

2 T. apple cider vinegar
2 T. mayonnaise (or yogurt)
1/4 tsp. salt
2 c. coarsely grated fresh
  carrot

3/4 c. coarsely grated apple
2 T. chopped walnuts or
  almonds (optional)
2 T. raisins (optional)

In the bottom of a large bowl, whisk together vinegar, mayonnaise, and salt. Add other ingredients and toss. Serves 4 to 6 as a side dish.

Margie Paskert
Barklee Farm
Sagle, Idaho

# CARROT, SQUASH & PARSNIP SOUP
## (This soup was a hit at our CSA Farm Day!)

2 T. olive oil
3 large leeks, white and tender
  green parts only, rinsed well,
  thinly sliced
3 c. peeled and diced butternut
  squash
3 c. thinly sliced carrots

1 c. thinly sliced parsnips
6 c. water, vegetable or chicken
  stock
1/4 tsp. fresh ground pepper
1/4 tsp. nutmeg
salt, to taste

Heat olive oil in pan over medium-low heat. Add leeks and sauté, stirring slowly for 10 minutes. Add squash, carrots and parsnips. Cook uncovered for 7 to 8 minutes, stirring occasionally. Add water or broth, pepper, and nutmeg and bring to boil. Reduce heat to low and simmer covered for 30 minutes or until vegetables are tender.

**Recipe Note:** Other varieties of winter squash or root vegetables can easily be substituted when making this delicious vitamin-packed soup.

Matthew Kurek
The Golden Earthworm Organic Farm
Jamesport, Long Island, New York

# Zesty Carrots

12 carrots (2 pounds, peeled and thinly sliced)
1/4 c. water
4 T. horseradish
1 c. mayonnaise
1/2 tsp. black pepper
1/2 tsp. salt
2 T. chopped onion
buttered bread crumbs

Microwave the carrots in water until tender. Then drain. Mix the horseradish, mayonnaise, salt, pepper, and onion. Add this mixture to the carrots; turn to coat. Place in an ovenproof casserole dish and cover with buttered bread crumbs. Bake at 350 degrees until heated through, about 15 minutes.

Maureen Baptiste
Pitcher Mountain CSA
Stoddard, New Hampshire

# Maple Glazed Carrots

8 medium carrots
3 T. butter
1/4 c. pure Vermont maple syrup
1/4 tsp. ginger (optional)

Slice carrots. Cook until tender. Drain. Add maple syrup and butter. Simmer carrots in maple syrup mixture until glazed. Serves about 8.

Sara Schlosser
Sandiwood Farm
Wolcott, Vermont

65106-05

# GLAZED CARROTS

12 small carrots, cut
   diagonally, thinly sliced
2 T. melted butter
a dash of soy sauce

1 T. chopped garlic
2 T. or more of honey
3 T. chopped fresh basil

Steam carrots until "al dente." Prepare a saucepan with melted butter, a dash or two of soy sauce, and chopped garlic. Cook on medium-low heat. After all other ingredients are melted/cooked, add honey and chopped, fresh basil. Stir in the steamed carrots and mix well until all the pieces are covered with the glaze.

Bill Brammer III
Be Wise Ranch CSA
San Diego, California


# BUMPS' CARROT CASSEROLE
## (Carrots with cheddar!)

4 c. sliced carrots
1 T. grated or finely chopped
   onion
1/2 c. grated cheddar cheese

2 T. mayonnaise
10 salted crackers, crumbled
pepper

Boil carrots until tender. Drain carrots well and mash with a potato masher. Add remaining ingredients and mix well. Put into oiled baking dish and bake at 350 degrees for 20 to 25 minutes.

Patricia Carpenter
Eatwell Farm
Dixon, California

# CARROT GINGER SOUP

1 onion, chopped
1 T. olive oil
3 T. butter
2 small potatoes, diced
1 lb. carrots, diced

4 c. vegetable stock
2 T. minced fresh ginger
1 c. milk
salt and pepper, to taste

Sauté onion in oil and 2 tablespoons of butter for 3 to 4 minutes in a large saucepan. Add potatoes for a few minutes, then add carrots. Fry over low heat for 3 to 4 minutes, then cover and simmer for 10 minutes, stirring occasionally. Add veggie stock, bring to a boil and simmer until carrots/potatoes are tender. Sauté ginger lightly in remaining butter and add to soup. Purée soup in food processor, stir in milk, add salt and pepper and serve.

Joel Pitney
Winter Green Farm
Noti, Oregon

# PARSNIP CRISPS

## (Gain a new appreciation for parsnips!)

parsnips, cut into French fry
  sized pieces

olive oil
sea salt

Toss parsnips with olive oil and sea salt. Spread out on a cookie sheet and bake at 400 degrees for about 40 minutes or until crispy on the outside and tender on the inside.

Nancy Vail
Center for Agroecology & Sustainable Food Systems
UC Santa Cruz Farm & Garden

*"You can bury a lot of troubles digging in the dirt."*

Author Unknown

65106-05

# GRILLED NEW POTATO SALAD
## (Invite a friend over for a healthy lunch!)

2 lbs. good-sized new potatoes,
  scrubbed
1-2 T. olive oil
salt and pepper to taste
1/4-1/2 lb. fresh green beans

1/2 tsp. salt
1/2 pt. cherry tomatoes, whole
  or halved
Greek olives (as a garnish)

Toss potatoes, olive oil and salt in a baking dish. Roast at 375 degrees, covered, for 35 to 40 minutes. While potatoes are roasting, place the beans and salt in boiling water and cook until tender. Then rinse beans with cold water and set aside to drain. Once potatoes are roasted, cut them into halves or quarters of equal size. Place pieces on a hot grill (cut side down). Grill until golden brown. Toss potatoes, beans, and champagne vinaigrette in a bowl with cherry tomatoes. Serve spooned over a layer of salad greens. Garnish with Greek olives.

## Champagne Vinaigrette

2 T. champagne vinegar (or red
  wine vinegar)
6 T. olive oil

1/2 c. fresh basil
1/2 tsp. salt
1 garlic clove, coarsely chopped

In a blender, purée all ingredients until smooth.

Franz Rulofson, College of the Redwoods
Sustainable Agriculture Farm
Shively, California

# BABY POTATOES
## (This even tastes great as cold leftovers!)

whole tiny potatoes (enough to
  cover the bottom of a square
  or rectangular baking dish)
3-6 T. olive oil

1-3 tsp. salt
2-4 tsp. coarsely ground black
  pepper

Place potatoes on bottom of square or rectangle baking dish. Sprinkle with the olive oil, salt and pepper. Roll until potatoes are evenly coated. Bake at 350 degrees, uncovered for 30 to 60 minutes (depending on the size of potatoes).

**Recipe Note:** Bigger potatoes can be substituted if they are cut into small pieces, but they don't quite have the special texture as the baby potatoes!

Franz Rulofson, College of the Redwoods
Sustainable Agriculture Farm
Shively, California


# DILLED POTATO SALAD
## (Perfect for a picnic!)

5-6 waxy medium potatoes like
  Yukon Gold
1 c. crunchy veggies (cucumber,
  radishes, celery)
1 large onion

1 c. mayonnaise
3 tsp. yellow mustard
1 tsp. salt
1 tsp. pepper
1/4 c. minced fresh dill ferns

Boil, peel, and cube potatoes. Grate and add crunchy veggies (cucumber, radishes, celery). Chop and add onion. Stir in mayonnaise, yellow mustard, salt, pepper, and fresh dill ferns. Chill and adjust seasonings to taste.

Anne Morgan
Lakes & Valley CSA/Midheaven Farms
Park Rapids, Minnesota

65106-05

# LEEK AND POTATO CHOWDAH
## (Great on a cold day!)

3 large leeks
2 T. unsalted butter
3 c. vegetable stock
3 medium-large potatoes or
  6-7 medium finger potatoes,
  peeled and finely chopped
1 tsp. sea salt

Generous seasoning of freshly
  ground peppercorns
1-1/4 c. milk
1/4 c. sour cream
minced chives for garnish
5-6 drops Tabasco or other
  hot sauce (optional)

In a large stockpot, heat the butter over medium heat. Sauté the leeks until tender 10 minutes. Don't let them brown! Add stock, potatoes, salt, pepper and bring to a boil. Partially cover the pot and cook for 20 minutes or until the potatoes are tender. Purée 2/3 of the soup in a blender or food processor and return to the pot. Stir in the milk, sour cream and hot sauce. Reheat until hot but do not boil. Garnish with chopped chives. Serves 3 as a main dish.

Bonnie Biller
St. Martin de Tours Organic Farm
Palermo, Maine

# Merck forest summer potato salad

(Delight in the flavors of garlic and basil!)

6 garlic cloves
3 lbs. small potatoes
2 sweet red peppers
3 T. olive oil

salt and pepper, to taste
3 T. balsamic vinegar
fresh basil, to taste

Wrap garlic in foil. Halve potatoes and dice peppers and toss them with 3 tablespoons olive oil, salt and pepper. Bake at 350 degrees for 35 minutes or until potatoes are tender and golden brown. Roast wrapped garlic simultaneously. In a bowl, toss hot potatoes and peppers with 2 tablespoons vinegar and cool. Remove garlic from foil and squeeze pulp into small bowl. Mash garlic with remaining vinegar and add to potatoes. Add basil just before serving. Best served at room temperature or chilled.

Linda McLenithan
Merck Forest & Farmland Center CSA
Rupert, Vermont


# Simple potato bake

(An easy but irresistible side dish.)

10-12 medium potatoes, unpeeled, cooked, drained and mashed
8 oz. package of cream cheese
1 small tub of sour cream

1 tsp. salt
1-2 cloves of crushed garlic
1 medium onion, sautéed
½ lb. broccoli, carrots, or other veggies

In a skillet sauté an onion, garlic and other veggies. Mix together cream cheese, sour cream, salt and mashed potatoes until well blended. Mix potato mixture and veggies in a 9 x 13 pan. Bake at 350 degrees until veggies are soft.

Michele Conyer
The White Violet Center for Eco-Justice
Saint Mary of-the-Woods, Indiana

65106-05

# POTATO-LEEK SOUP
## (A flexible and forgiving recipe)

3 medium leeks, white and
  green parts only, rinsed
  thoroughly to remove all dirt
  and then diced
small amount of butter, to
  sauté the leeks
3-4 medium potatoes,
  scrubbed and diced

3-4 c. chicken or vegetable
  broth
milk or cream
white pepper
nutmeg

Sauté leeks in butter until translucent. Simmer potatoes in broth until tender (about 20 minutes). Add leeks to potatoes and broth, allow to cool a bit. Purée soup mixture in a blender thinning with milk or cream as desired. Return to pan and heat through, adding white pepper and nutmeg to taste.

**Recipe Note:** Garnish each bowl of soup with sautéed red pepper. The pepper adds a festive touch to the soup and it tastes great too!

Justine and Brian Denison
Denison Farm
Schaghticoke, New York

# MASHED POTATOES AND TURNIPS

1 lb. turnip
1 lb. potatoes
milk, for desired texture
1-3 T. butter
2-3 cloves of garlic or ginger
  (optional)

salt and pepper, to taste
1 stalk of green onion or leek,
  chopped

Peel (optional) and cut turnips and potatoes into approximately 1-inch cubes. Boil gently until tender, about 12 to 15 minutes. Drain water and mash until smooth, adding milk and butter to desired texture and salt and pepper to taste. Sauté garlic or ginger (and a stalk of green onion or leek) in butter or olive oil for a few minutes to soften and add to potato mixture.

Todd Schulte
Eatwell Farm
Dixon, California


# SAGE POTATO THINS

3 medium potatoes
1/2 c. sliced fresh sage
1-2 T. olive oil
salt and pepper, to taste

1/4 c. grated Parmesan cheese
  (optional)
1/4 c. crumbled bacon, cooked

Line cookie sheet with parchment and spray or lightly brush with olive oil. Cut potatoes length-wise in 1/8 inch slices and lay half on the cookie sheet. Layer sage, salt, pepper, cheese and bacon on potato slices. Top with another potato slice and spray or brush with olive oil. Bake at 400 degrees for 20 to 30 minutes or until slightly golden brown, flipping once to brown both sides. Serve hot.

Sarah Wu-Norman
Merck Forest & Farmland Center CSA
Rupert, Vermont

65106-05

# GRANDMA KERESTES' CREAMED RADISHES

## (Kids love eating radishes prepared like this!)

4 T. butter
4 T. flour
1 c. milk
salt and freshly ground black
  pepper, to taste

1 large bunch red radishes,
  cleaned and thinly sliced

Melt butter in saucepan over low heat. Stir in flour. Cook over medium heat, stirring constantly, until mixture is smooth and bubbly. Remove from heat. Gradually stir in milk. Heat to a boil, stirring constantly. Add salt and pepper to taste. Boil and stir one minute. Meanwhile, steam radishes to desired firmness (approximately 5 minutes). Fold sauce into steamed radishes.

**Recipe Note:** Steaming the radishes take away any bitterness leaving a sweet vegetable, more delicately flavored than carrots or other roots.

Jody & Beth Osmund
Cedar Valley Sustainable Farm CSA
Ottawa, Illinois

# FRENCH BREAKFAST RADISHES

## (The rosemary-garlic butter makes these delicious!)

1 stick butter (either salted or unsalted), softened
1 (8-oz.) pkg. cream cheese, softened
4 tsp. chopped fresh rosemary (approx. 4 stems)
3 tsp. chopped fresh thyme
1 garlic clove, minced
salt, to taste
2 bunches French breakfast radishes, washed and tops trimmed

Mix all ingredients together except radishes. Cover and refrigerate for at least an hour or up to three days. Bring rosemary-garlic butter to room temperature before serving with radishes. (The garlic, rosemary, thyme and a little salt can be smashed together with a mortar and pedestal. The herb leaves will come off the stems and create a lovely chunky green paste to mix with the cream cheese and butter. The radishes can also be cut in half the long way and the rosemary garlic butter can be piped on each half and finished with a sprig of rosemary or thyme.)

**Recipe Note:** To substitute fresh herbs for dried herbs, follow the general rule of 3 teaspoons fresh = 1 teaspoon dried.

Amy Nichols, Clemson University
Calhoun Field Laboratory Student Organic Farm
Clemson, South Carolina

65106-05

# AFRICAN SWEET POTATO STEW
## (An exotic vegetarian stew!)

1 large onion, chopped
2 garlic cloves, minced
1 bunch of Swiss chard, stems
  and greens separated
6-8 plum tomatoes
1 hot pepper, minced (or a
  dash of hot pepper flakes)
1 (15-oz.) can garbanzo beans
½ c. raisins

2-3 large sweet potatoes,
  peeled and diced in ½ inch
  pieces
1 tsp. ground cumin
1 tsp. curry powder
1 tsp. salt
½ tsp. black pepper
½ c. couscous
2 c. water or chicken broth

Fry onion, garlic and white stems of chard until barely limp. Add tomatoes, minced hot pepper if using, and chopped greens. Fry a bit. Add garbanzo beans, raisins, sweet potatoes, cumin, curry powder, hot pepper flakes, salt and pepper. Cook 3 to 5 minutes. Use a large spoon to make a deep well in the center of the mixture in the pot. Put the couscous in the well and pat down until couscous is wet, adding water or chicken broth to cover if necessary. Cover tightly and simmer gently until couscous is cooked, about 25 minutes. Adjust seasoning.

Trish Mumme
Garden Patch Produce CSA
Alexandria, Ohio

# SWEET POTATO POT PIE
## (A delicious vegetarian dinner!)

### Filling

| | |
|---|---|
| 2 c. lentils | 1 onion, chopped |
| 6 c. water | 1 tsp. ground cinnamon |
| 1 T. grated ginger | 1 tsp. ground cumin |
| 3 garlic cloves, minced | 1 tsp. ground coriander |
| 1 c. canned crushed tomatoes or tomato purée | 1 tsp. sea salt |

### Bottom Layer

| | |
|---|---|
| 3 c. water | 1 tsp. sea salt |
| 1 T. olive oil | 1 c. polenta |

### Top Layer

| | |
|---|---|
| 6 yams, baked until soft | ½ tsp. sea salt |

Boil the lentils in a saucepan. Add other filling ingredients and cook until the lentils are soft. Make the bottom layer by boiling water and adding oil and salt. Then add polenta slowly stirring until it thickens. Put in the bottom of your baking dish and let cool. For the top layer, peel and mash the yams and add the sea salt. When the lentils are done. Pour them over the polenta and then smooth the yams on top. Bake at 350 degrees for 15 minutes or until the dish is heated through.

Jonathan Kirschner
Holcomb Farm CSA
West Granby, Connecticut

*"The greatest gift of the garden is the restoration of the five senses."*
*Hanna Rion*

65106-05

# CURRIED SWEET POTATO SOUP

1 T. olive oil
1 large onion, chopped
2 large garlic cloves, finely
  chopped
3 tsp. curry powder
1 large sweet potato, peeled
  and cubed
2 small to medium white
  potatoes, peeled and cubed
1 carrot, chopped into small
  pieces

1 small head of broccoli, broken
  into small pieces
1 celery stalk, chopped into
  small pieces
1 kale leaf, finely chopped
1 large apple, peeled, cored and
  finely chopped
6 c. chicken stock
ground black pepper, to taste

Heat the oil in a large stockpot and cook the onion over medium heat for 10 minutes, stirring occasionally, until very soft. Add the garlic and curry powder and cook for one more minute. Add all of the remaining ingredients and stir to mix. Bring to a boil and reduce the heat to simmer, partially covered for 30 minutes or until the sweet potato is very soft. If desired, allow the soup to cool a little and then purée some of the potatoes in a food processor until smooth and then return to the stockpot for a creamy soup.

**Recipe Note:** This is such a delicious and nutritious soup when made with organic vegetables and cage-free organic chicken broth. If you are a curry and veggie lover, you are sure to enjoy this soup! -Darlene

Darlene Kohler
Temple Wilton Community Farm
Wilton, New Hampshire

# POCKET SWEET POTATOES

6 tiny sweet potatoes                    butter
garlic cloves, peeled and
  chopped

Wash and scrub ½ dozen tiny sweet potatoes (usually about 5 inches long and a few inches in diameter), poke them with a fork, and bake them directly on the rack in the oven at 375 degrees for 20 to 30 minutes. (If overcooked, sweet potatoes are very forgiving.) Then slip some slivers of garlic and butter into a few of them to eat immediately, and leave the rest in the refrigerator to eat for lunch the next day. Sweet potatoes are even sweeter when they're cold and can be easily reheated, even in the microwave.

**Recipe Note:** When we grow sweet potatoes, our members are quick to take the mid-sized potatoes, leaving behind crates of the tiny and huge sweets. This is a mystery to me, because the huge ones store the longest, and the tiny ones are easiest for me to cook! I keep hot-mini sweets in my pockets to keep me warm if I'm too busy to break for lunch! -Carrie

Carrie Vaughn
Clagett Farm CSA
Upper Marlboro, Maryland

65106-05

# Sweet potato fries

sweet potatoes, peeled and
  sliced

salt, to taste

vegetable oil, enough to coat
  the bottom of a pan

## Deep Frying Method

Heat vegetable oil in deep fryer or deep frying pan. Add potatoes. Fries
are done when they rise to the top; they will be crispy on the outside, and
tender on the inside. Sprinkle with salt or seasoned salt, as desired.

## Baking Method

Boil the sweet potatoes until just nearly soft, not mushy. Cut into
fries or wedges. Sprinkle with vegetable or olive oil. Place on a cookie
sheet and bake at 400 degrees until crispy on the outside. Sprinkle
with salt or seasoned salt, as desired.

**Recipe Note:** These fries are a particular favorite of children, who are
always surprised at the unexpected sweetness!

Asha Dobbs
Clagett Farm CSA
Upper Marlboro, Maryland

# JULIE'S ROASTED SWEETS
## (Absolutely addictive!)

5-6 sweet potatoes, peeled
and cut into 1 inch chunks
1 sweet onion, peeled and
chopped
1 tsp. fresh ground black
pepper

1 tsp. garlic powder
4 T. extra virgin olive oil
1 lb. fresh beets, peeled and
cut into 1 inch chunks
(optional)

Place potatoes and onions in a shallow baking dish. Sprinkle with seasonings and oil. Mix well in the pan. Bake uncovered at 375 degrees for 40 to 50 minutes or until potatoes are soft and browned. Stir mixture once after baking for 25 minutes.

**Recipe Note:** These potatoes will take you from a summer BBQ to a Thanksgiving dinner. Let them cool slightly; they are great in a garden salad with a raspberry vinaigrette! Add peeled fresh beets to the sweet potato mixture before baking for a vibrant display!

Julie Sochacki

# NATURALLY SWEET POTATOES

6 sweet potatoes, peeled, par-
boiled, and sliced ½ inch
thick
1 (20-oz.) can crushed
pineapple

2 c. orange juice
½ c. brown sugar
¼ c. cornstarch
½ tsp. salt
grated orange peel

Lay potatoes in 3 domino type rows in a greased casserole dish. Combine all other ingredients to make a glaze. Pour glaze over potatoes and bake at 350 degrees for 30-45 minutes.

John Dysinger
Bountiful Blessings Farm
Williamsport, Tennessee

65106-05

# Turnips and Pears

1 lb. hakurei turnips
3 pears
unsalted butter
1 onion, peeled and sliced thinly

²/₃ c. walnut, halves
salt and pepper, to taste
½ lemon
fresh chopped parsley

Cut turnips in half, then into ¼ inch thick slices. Cut pears in half, core and cut into ¼ inch thick slices. Sauté turnips in butter until tender and crisp. Add pears and onions. Cook while stirring mixture for about 3 minutes. Add walnuts. Cook for 2 minutes. Season with salt and pepper. Squeeze lemon over mixture and sprinkle with parsley.

Eileen Droescher
Ol' Turtle Farm
East Hampton, Massachusetts

# Turnip Fries

## (A creative alternative to potato fries!)

turnips, peeled and chopped
  into French-fry strips

olive oil
sea salt

Lightly coat turnip strips with olive oil. Place on a flat baking sheet and sprinkle with sea salt. If desired, also sprinkle with your favorite herbs and spices. Bake at 350 degrees for 20 minutes.

**Recipe Note:** Add any of the following herbs and spices before baking the turnips: ground pepper, cayenne pepper, dried parsley, and/or dried basil.

Nancy Vail
Center for Agroecology & Sustainable Food Systems
UC Santa Cruz Farm & Garden

# TOM'S BEET AND TURNIP RISOTTO

1 bunch or 1 pound turnips
1 bunch or 1 pound beets
2 medium carrots
1 bunch green onions
up to 3 pounds greens-any
   combo of chard, spinach,
   beet and turnip greens
juice of one lemon
2 T. butter
2 T. olive oil
2 c. Arborio rice

1 T. fresh thyme or 1 teaspoon
   dried
2-1/2 c. dry white wine
8 c. stock
1 T. dried basil
grated Parmesan or Romano
   cheese (optional)
chopped fresh parsley
   (optional)
salt and freshly ground pepper,
   to taste

Peel the turnips if they're purple topped. White turnips don't need to be peeled. Scrub the beets and carrots. Chop the beets, turnips, and carrots into a small dice. Slice the onions at about 1/4 inch intervals. Clean the greens and roughly chop. Juice the lemon and set aside. Have a pot of stock simmering, covered on the stove. Heat the butter and olive oil over medium heat in a large, heavy pot. Add the rice and thyme and stir for 1 minute to coat all the grains with oil. Add 2 cups of the wine, bring to a boil, and stir occasionally until liquid is absorbed. Now add 2 cups stock and all the greens and vegetables. Stir well and simmer until all the liquid is absorbed. Add the basil. Now add 1/2 cup stock at a time, stirring constantly, waiting until all liquid is absorbed each time before adding more. You may not need all the stock. When the risotto is looking thick and the grains are clearish, taste for tenderness. It should be soft but not mushy. When it is nearly done, add another 1/2 cup of wine and stir until absorbed. Finish with lemon juice to taste. Salt and pepper, to taste. Each portion may be topped with cheese and parsley. Serve with a crunchy salad and warm bread.

**Recipe Note:** I find that regular beet risotto is too sweet, so I developed this recipe with half beets, half turnips, and lots and lots of greens. It's still a beautiful red. The turnips add their smoky complexity without overpowering. -Tom

Tom McElderry
Eatwell Farm
Dixon, California

65106-05

# SHARE SOUP

## (Clean out last week's share with this puréed soup!)

**Soup Base (some or all of these veggies)**

1 qt. water or more to cover veggies
1 potato with skin
tops of 2 bunches of celery
top ⅓ of 3 leeks (trimmed a little and washed well)
½ onion, chopped
3 carrots
handful of turnips
parts of two fennel bulbs (save some for chopping into the soup)

5 collard leaves, removed from the stems
½ winter squash (peeled and chopped)
1 bunch parsley
your favorite seasonings or: garlic, salt, pepper, cumin, ground coriander, crushed red pepper
1 bay leaf

Simmer until veggies are tender to well-done and purée in blender adding additional liquid if necessary. Return to pot.

**Featured Veggies**

one shares worth of carrots, turnips, fennel, celery and leek bottoms
1 onion, chopped
2 lbs. potatoes, diced
Swiss chard, stems and leaves separated
parsley, chopped

cilantro, chopped
1 cup of uncooked lentils or 1 cup of cooked beans, per targeted serving
lime juice, lemon juice, cider vinegar or cooking wine (for a kick!)

Fill your soup pot with chopped veggies and uncooked lentils or cooked beans. Cover these items with the soup base adding water if necessary. Cook for about 20 minutes or until everything is tender. Add chopped greens and remaining ingredients during last 5 minutes or so. Taste and adjust seasonings.

(continued)

**Recipe Note:** While all this is simmering you can clean the kitchen, put away this week's share or chop the featured veggies for the soup. Just keep adding veggies and seasonings until you have the amount and taste that you desire. Think of this as a work of art or a practical way of filling your belly, depending upon your mood! -Amy

Amy Sprague
Wolf Pine Farm
Alfred, Maine

# SPLIT PEA SOUP
## (Easy crockpot dinner for a cold day!)

1 bag of green split peas,
  rinsed well
10 c. water
3 celery stalks, chopped
1 medium onion chopped
2 carrots, shredded

6 medium red or Yukon gold
  unpeeled potatoes, diced
1 ($\frac{1}{2}$ pound) slice of ham, diced
  (optional)
1 T. freshly ground black pepper
2 tsp. garlic powder

Combine all ingredients in a slow cooker. Cook 5 to 6 hours on high or 10 to 11 hours on low. Mash soup with a potato masher before serving.

**Recipe Note:** Omit the ham for a delicious vegetarian dinner!

Julie Sochacki

65106-05

# ROOT VEGETABLE GRATIN WITH GORGONZOLA CHEESE

## (Excellent mix of flavors!)

3/4 lb. parsnip (1 large)
3/4 lb. rutabaga (1 large)
3/4 lb. carrot (3-4)
1-1/4 c. whipping cream (can substitute half and half for a little lighter dish)
1/2 c. chicken broth

4 garlic cloves, minced
1/2 tsp. fresh minced thyme (or 1/8 teaspoon dried)
4 oz. crumbled Gorgonzola cheese
1/2 tsp. salt
white pepper

Peel parsnips, rutabaga and carrots and cut into 1/4-inch-thick slices. Bring cream, stock, garlic and thyme to boil in large saucepan. Add rutabagas, cover and simmer 10 minutes. Add carrots and parsnips and simmer 5 minutes longer. Season with 1/2 teaspoon of salt and white pepper. Transfer vegetables and cream mixture to shallow baking dish. Bake at 425 degrees uncovered until vegetables are tender and liquid thickens, about 35 minutes. Sprinkle cheese over top and broil until golden. Cool 15 minutes before serving. Serves 4 to 5.

Solyssa Visalli
Cop Copi Farms
La Grand, Oregon

# ROOT VEGGIE CASSEROLE WITH CARAMELIZED ONIONS

7 c. low-sodium chicken or
   vegetable broth
3 lbs. yellow potatoes, peeled
   and cut into 1-1/2 inch pieces
1-1/2 lbs. rutabagas, peeled and
   cut into 1-1/2 inch pieces
1-1/4 lbs. parsnips, peeled and
   cut into 1-1/2 inch pieces

8 garlic cloves
1 bay leaf
1 tsp. dried thyme
3/4 c. butter, at room
   temperature
3 large onions, thinly sliced

Butter a 13 x 9 x 2-inch glass baking dish. Combine first 7 ingredients in a large pot; bring to boil. Reduce heat, cover partially and simmer until vegetables are very tender, about 30 minutes. Drain well. Transfer vegetables to a large bowl. Add 1/2 cup of butter. With electric mixer, beat until mashed but still chunky. Season with salt and pepper. Transfer mashed vegetables to prepared dish. Melt remaining 1/4 cup butter in a large, heavy skillet over medium-high heat. Add sliced onions and sauté until beginning to brown, about 5 minutes. Reduce heat to medium low and sauté until onions are tender and golden brown, about 15 minutes. Season with salt and pepper. Spread onions evenly over mashed vegetables. (Casserole can be prepared up to one day ahead, if covered and refrigerated.) Bake casserole at 375 degrees uncovered until heated through and top begins to crisp, about 25 minutes.

**Recipe Note:** Variations: add chopped spinach and either mix into potato mixture or add a layer of cooked spinach, kale or mustard greens in the center of the casserole and cover with remaining potato mixture.

David Van Eeckhout
Hog's Back Farm
Arkansaw, Wisconsin

*"Heaven is beneath our feet as well as over our heads."*
*Henry David Thoreau*

65106-05

# ROASTED ROOTS
## (Use your favorite combination of root veggies!)

| | |
|---|---|
| beets | garlic |
| carrots | shallots |
| potatoes | winter squash |
| parsnips | olive oil/butter |
| leeks | garlic salt and pepper, to taste |
| onion | |

Use any combination of the vegetables listed above. Slice each vegetable ¼ inch thick. Grease 1 to 2 cookie sheets with olive oil and butter. Coat both sides of the veggies with the oil from the pan. Season with garlic salt and pepper. Roast veggies at 500 degrees for 10 minutes or until they begin to brown. Then flip the root vegetables and continue to roast for 5 to 10 minutes more.

Brian Denison
Denison Farm
Schaghticoke, New York

**Recipe Favorites**

# Recipe Favorites

65106-05

# GREENS

# GREENS

## ALL ABOUT GREENS

Greens come in many different shapes, sizes and flavors, but all have one thing in common - they are largely composed of water. They are easy to keep fresh and delicious once you know the simple basics of handling and storing. Since most greens are grown in sandy soil, they require a bit more care in washing to remove the extra grit. Greens must be washed before eating or cooking.

### Store

All greens prefer a cool, moist (but not wet) environment. Store sturdier greens like kale and mustards loosely wrapped in plastic or vegetable storage bags in the crisper section of the refrigerator. The crisper section has high humidity, so vegetables should last a little longer when stored there. For lettuces, invest in a salad spinner. You will not regret it! Look for one with a bowl, spinner top and internal basket (avoid spinners with drainage holes). Lettuce may be stored unwashed, but it is easy to wash and store right in the spinner, ready-to-eat at a moment's notice.

### Wash

With the exception of lettuce greens, do not wash greens until just before using. This wash method seems tedious, but the extra few minutes is worth it to avoid crunching down on a mouthful of grit and sand: Fill a tub or bucket with cool water. Separate head of greens into leaves and swish around in the water. Hold leaves against the side of the tub and wait for the grit to settle at the bottom. Discard water (good for watering house plants). Repeat at least another time or two until no grit settles at the bottom of the tub.

(continued)

## Prepare

The greens from CSA farms are generally so fresh and tender that the stems can be eaten along with the leaves. If you do not like stems, or if they seem a little tough, remove them: fold the leaf in half lengthwise along the stem. Hold the stem firmly in one hand and tear the leaves off with the other hand. Leaves of sturdier greens may be left whole, torn, or cut into strips for cooking. Lettuce will stay crisp longer and hold up to dressings better when leaves are torn rather than cut.

Susie Wood
Provident Farm
Bivalve, Maryland

# ARUGULA AND POTATO SOUP

## (A delicious way to use your stale bread!)

3 c. water
4 medium potatoes, peeled and
  diced
2 c. loosely-packed arugula
  leaves

2 pinches of salt
2 c. stale Italian or French
  bread, cut into cubes
¼ c. green, fruity olive oil
freshly ground pepper, to taste

Combine water and potatoes in a soup pot; boil for 15 minutes. Add arugula and 2 pinches of salt. Cover and cook about 20 minutes at medium heat. Remove from heat and add bread. Cover and let stand for 10 minutes. Add olive oil and pepper. Stir well and serve immediately.

the Nye/Williams family
Denison Farm
Schaghticoke, New York

# ARUGULA, PEAR AND PECAN SALAD
## (With blue cheese dressing or ginger vinaigrette)

3 c. arugula leaves, washed
with stems removed (other
greens can also be added
with the arugula)
1 Bosch pear, chopped

3 T. blue cheese vinaigrette
dressing or a ginger
vinaigrette
½ c. chopped pecans, toasted

Toss arugula, pears and dressing together in a large bowl. Top with toasted pecans and serve.

**Recipe Note:** Eat this salad with a delicious vegetable soup for a satisfying meal. Our neighbor and farm friend, Chrissy, also used this recipe with fresh golden roasted beets from our farm. The beets were so sweet that we couldn't tell the difference between the beets and the pears! -Annaliese and Jared

Annaliese Franz & Jared Shaw
Waltham Fields Community Farm
Waltham, Massachusetts

# BEET GREENS WITH GINGER AND HOT PEPPERS

1 large bunch beet greens, about ¾ lb.
half to whole hot green pepper, about 2-3 inches long

1 inch piece fresh ginger root
1 T. oil, peanut or vegetable
4 T. water
salt, to taste

Wash greens thoroughly and shake but do not dry. Remove stems and keep leaves whole or cut into thin ribbons. Slice pepper in half and remove stem, seeds and white pith. Mince finely to make about 2 to 3 teaspoons. Peel ginger and slice very thinly. Stack slices together and cut into small matchsticks. In a large, nonstick pan, heat oil over medium-high heat until hot, but not smoking. Add ginger and hot pepper. Stir-fry for about a minute. Add beet greens and heat and stir until wilted. If no liquid remains in the pan, add a tablespoon or two of water; cover pan. Steam for another few minutes until greens are tender. Remove lid and stir to evaporate liquid, watching carefully so that greens do not burn. Season with salt, if desired. Serves 4.

**Recipe Note:** To preserve the color of the greens and keep them from turning brown or gray, add salt at the end of the cooking process. Caution: Wash hands well and don't rub eyes after touching or cutting a hot pepper!

Susan Brazer
Provident Farm
Bivalve, Maryland

65106-05

# BARBARA'S BEETS AND BEET GREENS SALAD

1 bunch beets with tops and
  stems, at least 1 lb.
3 T. oil, olive or canola
1 onion, chopped
2 garlic cloves, chopped

Italian seasonings
1 can garbanzo beans
Italian salad dressing
  (optional)
lemon, optional

Wash beets and greens. Separate greens and beets and save greens and beet stems. Boil beets until soft and allow to cool. Heat oil in a large skillet. Chop beet stems into 1 inch long pieces. Sauté them in a skillet for 3 minutes. Add onion and garlic and sauté for 5 minutes until onion is transparent. Add 2 teaspoons of Italian seasoning. Chop beet greens into large bite-sized pieces. Add beet greens to pan and sauté until wilted but still bright green. Add garbanzo beans. Chop cooked beets and add to mixture. Season with salt and pepper to taste. Add juice of ½ lemon if desired. May serve warm or cold. If serving cold, may use it as a cold salad and dress with Italian dressing. Stores for up to a few days in refrigerator.

Barbara Bosso
Holcomb Farm CSA
West Granby, Connecticut

# ASIAN HOT-SWEET BROCCOLI RAAB SALAD

1 bunch of Broccoli Raab, tough
  bottom 2 inches of stems
  discarded, very coarsely
  chopped and washed
1 bunch of radishes, washed,
  trimmed and sliced
2 carrots, sliced
2 T. olive oil, corn oil or peanut
  oil

1/4 tsp. red pepper flakes
1 clove garlic, minced (optional)
1 tsp. minced fresh ginger
  (optional)
1/4 c. chopped unsalted
  peanuts (optional)

Wash and slice all vegetables. Place large fry pan on medium heat. Add 2 tablespoons olive oil or other mild vegetable oil and heat until hot but not smoking. Add red pepper flakes, ginger and garlic and stir briefly until barely golden. Add carrots and radishes and cook about 3 to 5 minutes until still crisp and tender. Add broccoli raab, season with salt and pepper and cook briefly until green color intensifies and broccoli raab just begins to wilt. Add vegetables to bowl with dressing and toss to coat. Enjoy immediately or allow to cool, refrigerate to develop flavors. Salad keeps for 3 days, refrigerated.

## Dressing

1 T. sweet sherry, sweet
  vermouth or Japanese Mirin
1 T. cider vinegar or balsamic
  vinegar
1-1/2 T. honey

2 T. Asian sesame oil,
  preferably toasted or dark
1 T. soy sauce
salt and pepper to taste

Mix all dressing ingredients in a medium bowl until well combined. Pour over salad.

**Recipe Note:** This salad is just as good without the garlic, ginger and peanuts. Red bell pepper and green onions are also nice additions. Other greens such as mustard, kale and collards may be substituted for the broccoli raab.

Amy Nichols, Clemson University
Calhoun Field Laboratory Student Organic Farm
Clemson, South Carolina

65106-05

# ELAINE'S MOM'S BROCCOLI RAAB

broccoli raab
2 garlic cloves, chopped

1-3 tsp. olive oil
salt, to taste

Trim off a bit of the ends and wash the broccoli raab. In a sauce pan sauté a clove or two of chopped garlic with 1 to 3 teaspoons of olive oil until garlic begins to brown. Add chopped broccoli raab, with the water still clinging to its leaves, cover and simmer; add more water if it gets dry. Add salt to taste. Cook until the greens are tender. Serve with crusty bread to soak up the juices, or toss with pasta and Parmesan cheese.

Elaine Granata
Granata Farm
Denver, Colorado

# BROCCOLI RAAB OVER CAVATELLI

½ c. olive oil
1 big handful garlic scapes,
   chopped
½ lb. ground sweet Italian
   sausage (or meatless Italian
   sausage equivalent)
1 bunch scallions, sliced
   lengthwise and cut into 2
   inch pieces
1 bunch broccoli raab, stems
   cut into ½ inch pieces,
   leaves into 2 inch pieces

¼ c. white wine (optional)
1 lb. cavatelli (macaroni, usually
   found in frozen pasta section
   of market)
pepper and Romano cheese, to
   taste (absolutely required)
chili peppers or ground chili
   pepper, to taste (optional)

In a large sauté pan, heat the olive oil until warmed. Sauté garlic scapes for 5 minutes, then place the sausage in the pan and cook until the sausage has browned. Add scallions and broccoli raab, continue to simmer and stir. Add white wine and continue to cook until the wine has reduced slightly. Cook cavatelli according to package directions, drain well. Toss the pasta with the sauce. (Add some of the pasta water if the sauce is too dry.) Season with pepper and sprinkle with the Romano cheese.

**Recipe Note:** Neither Dr. Atkins nor the American Heart Association will approve of my recipe, but to a hyper-active Italian-American market farmer, this sure hits the spot! -Paul

Paul Bucciaglia
Fort Hill Farm
New Milford, Connecticut

*"Don't judge each day by the harvest you reap, but by the seeds you plant."*
*Robert Lewis Stevenson*

65106-05

# CHICORY TIAN

2-1/2 lbs. chicory
1/3 c. plus 3 tablespoons olive
  or canola oil
1 c. chopped onion
2-3 tsp. chopped garlic
1/2 c. sorrel leaves (optional)

sea salt
1/2 c. rice
3/4 c. grated Parmesan cheese
1/2 c. fresh bread crumbs
fresh ground pepper

Wash, dry and chop the chicory. In a large saucepan, heat 1/3 cup of the oil and cook the onions until clear, about 5 minutes. Add the garlic, stir for 30 seconds, then add the chicory, 1/2 pound at a time, stirring to coat with oil. Cook the chicory until slightly wilted. Add the sorrel (if using it), and cook until tender about 8 minutes. Meanwhile bring slated water to a boil, add rice and cook 5 minutes. Drain. When chicory is tender, lift from the pan and place in a bowl (approximately 5 cups). (Do not let chicory completely drain, because you will need some extra liquid to continue cooking the rice). Add the rice to the chicory, along with 1/2 cup cheese. Season the mixture with salt and pepper. Put in buttered 1-1/2 inch deep baking dish. Mix remaining cheese with the bread crumbs and sprinkle on top. Drizzle with remaining olive oil and bake at 400 degrees for 30 to 40 minutes. Serves 6 to 8.

Ann and Putnam Weekly
Maple Creek Farm
Yale, Michigan

# LEMON COLLARDS
## (simple and delicious)

1 bunch of collard greens,
  washed and cleaned
3 T. olive oil

1 dash of tamari sauce
the juice of one freshly
  squeezed lemon

Tightly roll a bunch of collards. Slice into thin strips. In a skillet, heat olive oil. Toss in collards and cook on high heat until done. Toss in tamari sauce and lemon juice. Serve immediately.

Nancy Vail
Center for Agroecology & Sustainable Food Systems
UC Santa Cruz Farm & Garden

# COLLARDS WITH PROSCIUTTO

½ c. diced prosciutto
3 T. butter
½ c. diced onions

2 tsp. minced garlic
2 lbs. fresh collard greens
3 c. chicken broth

Heat a large Dutch oven over medium-high heat; add prosciutto, and sauté 2 minutes. Add butter, onion, and garlic; sauté until onion is tender. Add greens and broth. Bring to a boil; reduce heat, and simmer 30 to 45 minutes or until greens are tender. Makes 10 cups.

Jennifer Smith
South Plains Food Bank
Lubbock, Texas

# KENYAN COLLARDS

1 T. olive oil
1 onion, chopped
2-3 tomatoes, chopped

1 bunch collard greens
salt, to taste

Sauté onion in olive oil. Add tomatoes to the onions. Stack the collard leaves and then roll them into a tight bunch. Cut collards finely into thin pieces. Steam with onion mixture until tender. Add salt to taste.

**Recipe Note:** We lived in Kenya for six years where Collard Greens, "Sikuma Wiki," are a staple in the average diet. Kale, chard or other greens can be substituted for collards in this recipe. -John

John Dysinger
Bountiful Blessings Farm
Williamsport, Tennessee

65106-05

# KATHY'S COLLARD GREENS

¼ lb. pork ground
1 T. olive oil
1 small onion, thinly sliced
1-2 garlic cloves, minced
1 inch knob of fresh ginger,
  peeled, thinly sliced and cut
  into thin strips
2 lbs. collard greens, washed,
  de-stemmed and cut into
  very thin strips, ⅛-¼ inch
  wide

1 can coconut milk
1 fresh jalapeño pepper, sliced
  into thin strips
salt, to taste
3-6 c. rice, fully cooked

Brown ground pork in olive oil. Add onion, garlic and ginger and sauté until they are softened. Add the collards and 1 can of coconut milk. Cook covered for about 15 minutes. Add sliced jalapeño and cook covered for another 15 minutes. Add salt to taste. Serve over rice.

Kathy Turner
Great Country Farms
Bluemont, Virginia

# POMELO-ESCAROLE SALAD

1 pomelo
1 Meyer lemon
1/4 tsp. salt
1/4 tsp. Dijon mustard
freshly ground black pepper
1/4 c. olive oil
1 watermelon radish, peeled and
   sliced or cut into thin
   julienne sticks

1/2 lb. lettuce, washed, torn,
   and dried
1 head escarole, cored and
   chopped

Section the fruits: cut a slice off the top and bottom, cutting a little bit into the sections. Then place the fruit on one end and cut down along the sides, removing the peel entirely, while saving as much fruit as possible. With fruit in hand, use a paring knife and cut along either side of each skin to free a skinless section. Remove all sections, then juice the remaining fruit into a bowl. Measure 2 tablespoons of juice. Add 1/4 teaspoon of salt, the mustard, and some black pepper. Now drizzle in the olive oil, whisking. Taste for salt by dipping a lettuce leaf. Marinate the radish in a little dressing for 1/2 hour. Ten minutes before serving, toss the escarole with some dressing. Place a handful of greens on each plate and top with the radish and citrus sections. Twist black pepper on top. Serves 4.

Tom McElderry
Eatwell Farm
Dixon, California

65106-05

# Kale and Kielbasa Soup

(Kielbasa gives this soup a rich, smoky flavor.)

3 T. olive oil
1-2 c. chopped onion or leek
1-2 c. chopped carrots
1-½ c. chopped celery with leaves
1-2 garlic cloves, chopped
2 large potatoes diced (or use 4-5 small potatoes)
1 bay leaf
4-5 c. chicken broth or vegetable broth

5-6 fresh tomatoes or 1 (28 oz.) can of tomatoes, undrained
6-8 oz. kielbasa, sliced in ¼ inch half moons
¼ c. chopped fresh parsley
1 bunch of fresh kale, stemmed and chopped
1 can of kidney beans, drained
salt and pepper, to taste

Sauté onion in olive oil. Add carrots, celery, and garlic. Sauté 1 minute more. Add potatoes, bay leaf, chicken broth, tomatoes, and kielbasa. Bring to boil until potatoes are soft. Add parsley, kale, and kidney beans. Cook a few more minutes. Season with salt and pepper. Serves 4 to 5.

**Recipe Note:** Omit the kielbasa and use vegetable broth, for a delicious vegetarian kale and bean soup.

Trish Mumme
Garden Patch Produce CSA
Alexandria, Ohio

# Kale crunch

olive oil spray
1 big bunch of kale, roughly cut
   into 2 x 2 pieces

3 T. grated Parmesan cheese

Line a cookie tray with foil. Spray the tray with olive oil spray or spread out a thin layer of olive oil across the pan with your fingers. Spread kale across pan. Bake at 350 degrees for 10 minutes, mixing once or twice. Sprinkle Parmesan over kale, and bake for a few more minutes, to taste. Cool on another plate or tray. The kale should be crispy and crunchy.

**Recipe Note:** CSA shareholder Alice Daood e-mailed me this recipe, by way of a friend from Belgium. She states that "it satisfies my urge for salty snacks." I say any recipe that can start with a bunch of kale and end with that statement has to be worth a shot! Thanks Alice! -Paul

Paul Bucciaglia
Fort Hill Farm
New Milford, Connecticut


# Kale with soy-garlic-olive oil sauce

## (compliments of Allison Adams)

5 c. torn kale
1-2 garlic cloves, minced
1 T. say sauce

1-1/2 tsp. olive oil
black pepper, to taste

Steam kale for 15 to 20 minutes in a large pot. Meanwhile, whisk together garlic, soy sauce, olive oil, and pepper. Drizzle dressing over greens while they're still warm.

Daniel Parson
Gaia Gardens
Decatur, Georgia

65106-05

# KALE CRUMBLE

1 bunch of kale leaves, stems
removed but leaves kept
whole
2 T. vegetable oil

salt, to taste
freshly grated Parmesan
cheese, to taste

Brush the kale leaves lightly with oil then sprinkle with salt and Parmesan. Put the leaves on a cookie tray and bake in the oven. Bake at 400 degrees until the leaves are as crispy as potato chips, about 10 minutes.

**Recipe Note:** Crumble them over rice, soup, salad or any dish where you want something crispy and salty.

Laura Sorkin
Cave Moose Farm
Cambridge, Vermont

# TUSCAN WHITE BEAN AND KALE SOUP
## (Great way to use that last bunch of Kale!)

2 (15-oz.) cans Cannellini beans
(small white beans), drained
and rinsed or 1-¼ cups dried
Cannellini beans
2 T. extra virgin olive oil
1 bay leaf
1 onion, diced
4 cloves of fresh garlic,
pressed or minced

2 carrots, diced
8 c. vegetable or chicken stock
1 bunch kale, washed, stemmed
and chopped into strips
1 (28 oz.) can of whole, peeled
tomatoes (discard juice and
chop into ½ inch pieces)
salt and pepper, to taste
Parmesan cheese (optional)

If using dry beans, sort and rinse beans in a large pot. Cover beans with 8 cups of cold water, stir and let stand for 8 hours or overnight. Heat olive oil over medium high heat for 1 minute. Reduce heat to medium and add bay leaf, onion, garlic, and carrots. Sauté vegetables until onion looks clear, approximately 5 minutes. (If vegetables begin to dry out or stick, add water to the pan.) Add stock to the pot. Add soaked beans, if using, and bring to a boil, skim top, reduce heat to simmer and cook gently, partly covered for 1-½ hours or until beans become soft and tender. If using canned beans, bring stock to boil, reduce heat to simmer, and add canned beans, chopped kale, and tomatoes. Simmer for 20 minutes. Add salt and pepper to taste. Add grated Parmesan cheese if desired.

Maggie Wood & Matthew Kurek
The Golden Earthworm Organic Farm
Jamesport, Long Island, New York

65106-05

# TANGERINE KALE

2 qts. kale, rinsed and
chopped, with coarser stems
removed

1 T. sesame seeds
a pinch cayenne powder
juice of one tangerine

Toast sesame seeds in a skillet. When seeds start dancing around in the pan and/or begin to change color, add the chopped kale. Unless the kale has quite a bit of water still clinging to the leaves, add a dash of water. Sprinkle the cayenne over the top and cover. Cook at moderate heat for 5 to 7 minutes or until kale is wilted. Empty the contents of the skillet into a serving bowl and drizzle tangerine juice over the top. Serve. (Even though we rotate through a variety of types of kale to provide visual interest, after a number of weeks kale can begin to wear out its welcome. That's when it's time for a special presentation that makes kale new all over again. In addition, the pairing in this recipe with citrus makes the minerals in kale more easily absorbed by the body, and the prep is quick and super easy.)

**Recipe Note:** This recipe comes from our gardening friend John Prescott in Canby, Oregon. Our CSA farm has a year round season, and during the winter months, kale is a frequent component of our harvest baskets. Kale once touched by a light frost becomes especially sweet and delicious and provides lots of vitamins and minerals as well. -John

John Martinson, Jr.
Birds & Bees Community Farm
Oregon City, Oregon

# ASIAN KALE

1 T. olive oil or butter
1 bunch of kale, washed and
  chopped
3 garlic cloves, chopped
2 T. minced onion
2 tsp. honey

2 tsp. apple cider vinegar
1 T. soy sauce
¼ c. water
2-4 servings of Basmati rice,
  fully cooked

Preheat a skillet coated with olive oil over medium high heat. Place kale, garlic, and onions in the skillet and sauté for about 4 minutes. Add all remaining ingredients and cover, cook gently for 10 minutes. Serve with Basmati rice. Serves 2 to 4.

Melinda Montgomery
Maple Creek Farm
Yale, Michigan

# KALE, LEEKS AND DILL

2 or 3 leeks, sliced lengthwise
  or across (or can use onions
  sliced in rings)
sesame oil
3-4 garlic cloves, finely chopped

1-2 bunches of kale, cut into
  large pieces
ume plum vinegar (or balsamic,
  brown rice, etc.)
dill, to taste

Caramelize leeks in oil. Add garlic and sauté lightly. Lower heat and add kale. Then add vinegar to taste and stir to mix leeks, kale and vinegar. Cover with lid and steam lightly. Add dill to taste, stir and re-cover with lid. Steam until kale is just bright green; do not overcook.

Eileen Droescher
Ol' Turtle Farm
East Hampton, Massachusetts

*"Reflect upon your blessings, of which every man has plenty, not on your past misfortunes, of which all men have some."*

Charles Dickens

65106-05

# BARLEY AND KALE GRATIN

²/₃ c. pearl barley
½ tsp. salt
1 large bunch of kale, stems
   removed
2 T. butter
3 T. flour

1-½ c. milk
¼ tsp. allspice
¼ tsp. grated nutmeg
salt and pepper, to taste
½ c. grated cheese (sharp
   cheddar or Asiago)

In a saucepan add the barley to 1 quart boiling water along with ½ teaspoon of salt, and simmer uncovered, until tender, 30 minutes. Drain. While the barley is cooking, cook the kale in a skillet of boiling salted water until tender, 5 minutes. Drain, reserving ¼ cup of cooking liquid. Purée the kale and its cooking liquid until smooth. Melt the butter in a small saucepan, whisk the flour, and then whisk in the milk. Cook, stirring constantly, over medium heat until thick. Season with allspice, nutmeg, salt and pepper. Combine all ingredients (barley, puréed kale, sauce and cheese) and check for seasoning. Transfer to a lightly buttered baking dish or ramekins. Bake at 375 degrees until lightly browned on top, 30 minutes.

**Recipe Note:** Variations: Use collards instead of kale, add cherry tomato halves and sweet onion, and use oregano and garlic instead of nutmeg and allspice in the sauce.

David Van Eeckhout
Hog's Back Farm
Arkansaw, Wisconsin

# PASTA AND KALE

1 bunch fresh kale, washed and
  chopped
1 garlic clove, minced
1/4 c. olive or vegetable oil
1 tsp. instant chicken flavored
  bouillon
1/2 tsp. chopped dried basil
  leaves or fresh

2 c. cottage cheese
1/2 tsp. salt
8 oz. pasta, cooked or drained
1/4 c. Parmesan and Romano
  cheese
1 T. chopped parsley

In a large skillet, cook kale and garlic in the oil for 5 minutes, stirring frequently. Dissolve bouillon in water recommended on package. Add bouillon mixture, basil, cottage cheese and salt to the kale. Stir over low heat until blended. Toss kale mixture, pasta, and grated cheese. Garnish with parsley.

Leigh Fosberry
Pitcher Mountain CSA
Stoddard, New Hampshire

65106-05

# KALE SOUP
## (This soup will warm you right up!)

3 garlic cloves, minced
1 large onion, chopped
3 T. olive oil
6 c. vegetable or chicken stock
2 c. finely chopped or puréed
   tomatoes

1 bunch shredded kale
1 can cannellini (white kidney)
   beans
Parmesan cheese
salt, pepper and herbs, to
   taste

Sauté garlic and onion in oil until translucent. Add stock and tomatoes. Heat to boiling. Add kale and cook on medium heat for about 20 minutes. Add cooked beans and heat. Sprinkle Parmesan on top when serving.

**Recipe Note:** One of the farm's favorite late Summer/ Fall recipes is Kale Soup from member Suzanne Dunn Krieg. For a smoother texture, process cooked soup in a blender or food processor before adding beans. Blend to desired consistency; then add cooked beans and heat.

Walter & Ellen Greist
Mill River Valley Gardens CSA
North Haven, Connecticut


# SPINACH-BASIL QUICHE

1-1/2 c. chopped spinach
1 T. herb butter
1/3 c. chopped onion
1-1/2 c. whole milk
3 eggs
1/8 tsp. black pepper

1 c. ricotta cheese
1/4 c. Parmesan cheese
1 T. chopped fresh African blue
   basil
2 c. cooked brown rice

Press rice in greased 8 x 8 pan. Sauté first three ingredients. Add remaining ingredients and heat to near boil. Pour over rice and bake at 425 degrees for 35 minutes.

Rusty & Claire Orner
Quiet Creek Herb Farm
Brookville, Pennsylvania

# SPINACH PIE

20 oz. fresh spinach, cleaned
  and chopped
3 T. olive oil
1 c. finely chopped onions
1 c. finely chopped leeks
1/4 c. butter
12 oz. feta cheese, crumbled

3/4 c. grated Parmesan cheese
1/4 c. finely snipped parsley
1 tsp. dried dill weed
24 sheets of frozen phyllo
  dough
3/4 c. unsalted butter, melted

In a large Dutch oven, cook spinach in hot oil until wilted, stirring occasionally. Remove from pan. Drain. In same pan, cook onions and leeks in the 1/4 cup butter until tender, but not brown. Stir together onion mixture, feta cheese, Parmesan cheese, parsley and dill. Blend the drained spinach into this mixture. Brush a large insulated baking sheet (or use two rimmed cookie sheets sandwiched together) with the unsalted butter. Place two sheets of the phyllo dough in the pan, and brush the dough with the butter. Repeat laying on the dough two sheets at a time and brushing with butter until you have placed and buttered half of the dough. Spread the spinach mixture on the dough as evenly as possible. Place two more sheets of phyllo dough on top of the spinach, and brush with butter. Repeat until you have used all the dough. If the dough hangs over the edge of the pan, trim with a knife after you've completely assembled the pie. Bake at 350 degrees for 50 to 55 minutes. The pie should be golden brown and should have shrunk away from the edges a bit. Serve and enjoy hot!

Theresa Williams
Pond House Farm CSA
Manton, Michigan

65106-05

# FRESH SPINACH BREAD BOWL DIP
## (Children love this dip!)

2 bunches of fresh spinach,
  cleaned, steamed and
  immediately rinsed with cold
  water
1 (16-oz.) container of low-fat
  cottage cheese

1 small clove of garlic minced
salt and pepper to taste
1 large Shepard's round loaf of
  bread

Mix cottage cheese, garlic, salt and pepper in a large bowl. Once spinach is cooled, chop and mix well with cottage cheese mixture. Place mixture in the refrigerator until ready to use. Take the round loaf of bread and cut out the top, as if you were carving a pumpkin. Remove the inside of the bread, so you have a half-inch shell. Shred inside and top of bread, bag and set aside for later use. When ready to serve, place spinach/cottage cheese mixture in the bread bowl. Serve with reserved bread chunks for dipping.

**Recipe Note:** As a child, this was a favorite recipe of Clifford William Lemasters, who passed away on September 19, 2004, at the age of 20 years. He is loved and thought of each day by his entire family. His mother Susan and sister Jessika remember how much he loved this dip. They hope others will use this dip to introduce more greens into childrens' diets.

Susan M. Gehrke and Jessika Lemasters
Be Wise Ranch CSA
San Diego, California

# JAY'S SPINACH AND MUSHROOMS

1 bunch spinach, approximately
   3/4 lb. (about 6 cups leaves,
   loosely packed)
2 T. olive oil
1 tsp. minced fresh garlic
12 oz. mushrooms - white
   button, portobella, shiitake
   or combination

1/2 tsp. salt
1/4 tsp. pepper
2 T. dry sherry or dry white
   wine
6-8 drops sesame oil
   (optional)
1/8 tsp. dried crushed red
   pepper (optional)

Wash spinach thoroughly and shake, leaving a few drops of water on the leaves. Remove stems, if desired, and set aside. Clean mushrooms. Cut portobella into thick slices and leave white button or shitake mushrooms whole. Heat oil over medium heat in large sauté or frying pan. Add garlic and sauté until fragrant but not brown, about a minute or two. Add mushrooms and increase heat to medium-high. Cook, stirring frequently, until mushrooms soften and become slightly caramelized. Stir in salt, pepper and sherry. Continue cooking until all moisture is evaporated. Add spinach to mushrooms and reduce heat to medium. Cook and stir just until spinach wilts. Taste and season with additional salt and pepper, if desired. Optional: If using sesame oil and crushed red peppers: after spinach has wilted, push vegetables to one side of pan. Add sesame oil and peppers to other side of pan and sauté for one minute. Stir into vegetables, taste and season with additional salt and pepper.

**Recipe Note:** Jay's daughter, Heather, who not too long ago went away to college, said one of the things she misses most about home is her dad's cooking. She requests this scrumptious vegetable dish when she returns from school.

Jay Martin
Provident Farm
Bivlave, Maryland

65106-05

# GREEK RICE WITH SPINACH
## (Lemon adds zest to this delicious rice dish.)

1-1/2 T. olive oil
1 large onion, chopped
2 cloves of garlic, minced
4 c. chopped clean, fresh
   spinach

3 T. lemon juice
4 c. cooked long grain rice
1-2 T. minced fresh basil
salt and pepper, to taste
1/4 c. crumbled feta cheese

In a skillet, add oil, onion and garlic. Cook on medium-high heat until onion is softened and transparent. Add spinach, lemon juice, and rice. Cook, stirring frequently, until spinach is limp and rice is thoroughly heated. Toss in basil. Add salt and pepper to taste. Add crumbled feta cheese before serving. Serves 4.

Kelly Saxer
Desert Roots Farm CSA
Queen Creek, Arizona

# SPINACH FRITTATA
## (Serves 20 as an appetizer or 8 as an entree)

2 T. butter or olive oil
1 small yellow onion, chopped
2 garlic cloves, finely chopped
4 green onions, thinly sliced on
   diagonal
6-8 oz. spinach

1 doz. eggs
1/2 lb. feta cheese
1/4 lb. grated Jack cheese
1/2 tsp. salt
1/4 tsp. pepper

Heat butter or oil in medium saucepan over medium heat. Add onion and garlic and cook until soft. Add green onions; cook a few minutes longer. Remove from pan. Add spinach to same pan, cook until wilted. Set aside to cool. Squeeze excess liquid out of spinach and chop coarsely. Break eggs into large bowl, whisk until blended. Add remaining ingredients. Pour into 3 qt baking dish or 9 x 13 inch baking pan. Bake at 350 degrees for about 30 minutes or until frittata is set. Serve warm, cold, or at room temperature. Tomato salsa goes wonderfully with this.

Marlene Washington
Eatwell Farm
Dixon, California

# INDIAN SPINACH SALAD

8 c. chopped spinach
1-1/2 c. chopped apple

1/2 c. golden raisins
1/2 c. walnuts

### Dressing

1/4 c. white wine vinegar
1/4 c. vegetable or canola oil
2 T. chutney
2 tsp. sugar

1/2 tsp. salt
1-1/2 tsp. curry powder
1 tsp. dry mustard
1 T. mustard seed

Combine all ingredients of dressing except oil. Slowly whisk to combine. Continue to briskly whisk while slowly adding the salad oil. Warm dressing just before serving so that it is warm but not hot. Chop walnuts roughly and toast until golden. Chop spinach roughly and place in salad bowl. Toss spinach with warm dressing. Top with apple, walnuts and raisins.

Solyssa Visalli
Cop Copi Farms
La Grand, Oregon

65106-05

# SPINACH LASAGNA

4 fresh eggs
salt and pepper, to taste
2 (16-oz.) cartons ricotta
  cheese
1 qt. homemade Italian tomato
  sauce (or 1 [32 oz.] jar of
  prepared spaghetti sauce)
4 fresh garlic cloves, minced
2 medium onions, chopped

$\frac{1}{8}$ tsp. cloves
32 oz. fresh spinach, chopped
2 c. grated cheddar cheese
2 c. grated mozzarella cheese
$\frac{1}{2}$ to 1 c. grated Parmesan
  cheese
1 (9-oz.) box of ready to bake,
  no boiling required, lasagna
  noodles

Grease a lasagna-sized baking pan. Prepare ricotta cheese mixture as follows: In medium sized bowl beat four eggs, add salt and pepper to taste, add 2 cartons of ricotta cheese. Mix well and set aside. Next, pour tomato sauce into pot and add the fresh minced garlic, one chopped onion, salt and pepper to taste, $\frac{1}{8}$ teaspoon cloves (or see fresh Italian sauce recipe below). Add one medium chopped onion to spinach, divide mixture in half, set aside for layering. Place 1 to 2 ladles of sauce in bottom of pan, layer uncooked noodles in bottom over sauce, and add half of spinach mixture over top of noodles. Add second layer of noodles, on top of spinach, add $\frac{1}{2}$ of the ricotta cheese mixture spreading gently over second noodle layer. Add third layer of noodles, and add remaining spinach over top. Add 4th layer of noodles, then add remaining ricotta cheese spreading thickly. Add 5th layer of noodles over top of ricotta and pour entire remaining sauce over top of last layer. Sprinkle all remaining cheese over top of last layer of sauce-covered noodles. It may appear watery, but do not drain. Noodles will soak up fluid. Pan will be very full, but will reduce when cooked. Bake covered at 365 degrees with foil for 50 minutes, remove foil and cook an additional 10 minutes. Remove from oven let cool 20 minutes before serving. Serves 8 or more.

(continued)

**Fresh Italian Tomato Sauce**

10 to 12 large tomatoes,
  chopped and slightly drained,
  remove seeds if desired
1 medium onion, chopped
1/8 tsp. oregano leaf

2-3 garlic cloves, minced
2 fresh basil leaves
2 tsp. sugar
pinch of cloves
salt and pepper, to taste

Simmer tomatoes on stove top for 20 minutes adding remaining ingredients. Stir frequently, until mixture reduces in size, cool a bit and set aside.

**Recipe Note:** Make ahead a day or so for the best flavor; cover with foil and place in your refrigerator. For a variation, mix 1/2 of the grated cheeses into the ricotta mixture and then top with remaining cheeses.

Ivy Sievers
Garden on the Prairie
Tama, Iowa

# Swiss chard pie

1 small onion chopped or sliced
  into rings
1/4 c. organic butter
30 leaves of Swiss chard cut
  into bite-sized pieces,
  discard stalks

2 eggs
1/2 c. grated cheese

Sauté onion in butter in large pot with the lid on. Put chard into the hot pan with no additional heat and cover until chard wilts, 1-2 minutes. Stir and put into a 9 inch glass pan. Break 2 eggs and stir on top with fork. Top with cheese and bake at 350 degrees until egg is firm. Optional, try several types of cheese, especially a goat-feta type cheese. The longer baked, the crispier it will become.

Tim P. Miller
Millberg Farm
Kyle, Texas

65106-05

# Swiss Chard and Caramelized Onion Calzone

1/4 c. vegetable oil
1 large onion, sliced
2 bunches of chard or kale,
   roughly chopped
1 T. chopped garlic
2 c. ricotta cheese

1/2 tsp. nutmeg
2 tsp. salt
1 tsp. pepper
1 lb. pizza dough, homemade or
   purchased
2 T. olive oil

Preheat oven to 450 degrees with pizza stone in the oven. Heat vegetable oil in a heavy skillet and add onion. Cook over medium heat, stirring frequently for 10 to 15 minutes until soft and browned. (If necessary, add a bit more oil or water to prevent onions from over-browning.) Add greens and garlic to the onions and cook 5 minutes or until greens are wilted. Cool greens and onion mixture 20 to 30 minutes until cool enough to handle. Squeeze any extra water from the greens. Mix ricotta with seasonings and add greens and onions. Adjust seasonings. Divide dough in half. For each half, roll the dough into a 10-inch circle. Drizzle dough with olive oil. Evenly spread half of the greens mixture over half of the 10-inch dough circle. Fold dough over the mixture and press to form a half-moon shape and crimp with thumbs. Bake 12 to 15 minutes or until golden. Serves 4.

**Recipe Note:** Enjoy these calzones with oven-roasted tomato sauce!

Ted McCormack and Wendy Crofts
Willow Pond Community Farm
Brentwood, New Hampshire

# CALABRESE SWISS CHARD
## (From the Italian region of Calabria)

6 T. olive oil, divided
½ medium onion, sliced or
  chopped
3 cloves of garlic, chopped or
  crushed
1 large bunch of Swiss chard
  (about 1-½ lb.)

⅓ lb. sliced bacon, cut into
  pieces and browned
½ c. grated Parmesan or
  Peccorino Romano cheese
bread crumbs

Blot grease from bacon, set bacon aside. Chop Swiss chard (stems about ½ inch thick, leaves larger). Sauté garlic in 2 tablespoons of oil. Add onion and sauté lightly. Add Swiss chard stems and cook 3 minutes, add leaves and cover. Cook 2 to 3 minutes. Mix cooked ingredients in a baking dish. Mixture should be about 2 inch deep in pan. Sprinkle bread crumbs over mixture and mix in lightly with a fork. Drizzle with remainder of olive oil. Bake at 350 degrees for 15 minutes. Then sprinkle with grated cheese and continue to bake until cheese is melted. Serves 8 to 10.

**Recipe Note:** I prefer to use ruby red Swiss chard for its sweeter, more beet-like flavor and for the beautiful red color which the juice takes from the red stems. I also prefer the robust flavor of hardneck garlic, either Korean Red Hot or Roja. -Bill

Bill Nunes
Contented Acres Produce
Gustine, California

*"If you hear a voice within you say, 'You are not a painter,' then by all means paint...and that voice will be silenced."*

*Vincent Van Gogh*

65106-05

# FRENCH-STYLE SWISS CHARD

**(Kale works just as well in this tasty dish.)**

1 T. olive oil
4 c. coarsely shredded Swiss
   chard

2 cloves of garlic, minced
4 T. grated Parmesan cheese

Heat a large, heavy skillet over medium-high heat. Add the olive oil, Swiss chard, and garlic. Sauté the mixture for 5 minutes or until the Swiss chard wilts. Sprinkle with cheese and serve immediately.

Kelly Saxer
Desert Roots Farm CSA
Queen Creek, Arizona


# SWISS CHARD FRITTATA

**(Share this frittata with friends for brunch!)**

1 onion, chopped
1 garlic clove, minced
2 T. olive oil
1/2 tsp. salt
1/2 tsp. basil
1/2 tsp. oregano
1/2 tsp. thyme
1/4 tsp. rosemary
freshly ground pepper, to taste

1 zucchini, chopped
1 bunch Swiss chard leaves,
   chopped
1 green bell pepper, chopped
mushrooms, sliced
5 eggs
1 c. shredded cheddar or
   grated Parmesan cheese

In a 9 or 10-inch cast iron skillet, sauté onion and garlic in olive oil with salt, basil, oregano, thyme, rosemary, and freshly ground pepper for 5 to 8 minutes. Add zucchini and Swiss chard leaves. If desired, add green bell pepper and sliced mushrooms. Beat 5 eggs and add shredded cheddar or Parmesan cheese. Turn heat up in frying pan. Pour egg-cheese mixture over veggies. Place pan in the oven at 400 degrees and cook for 12 to 15 minutes, or until it sets.

Anne Morgan
Lakes & Valley CSA/Midheaven Farms
Park Rapids, MN

# ANGEL HAIR PASTA WITH SWISS CHARD

1 T. olive oil
2 onions, thinly sliced
2 bunches Swiss chard, trimmed and chopped (about 14 cups)
4 garlic cloves, minced
1 (14-oz.) can diced tomatoes with juices
1/3 c. dry white wine
red pepper flakes, to taste
salt and pepper, to taste
8-10 oz. angel hair pasta
1/3 c. coarsely chopped pitted kalamata olives
4 T. freshly grated Romano cheese
1/2 c. chopped roasted red peppers

Heat the oil in a heavy large frying pan over medium heat. Add the onions and sauté until tender, about 8 minutes. Add the chard and sauté until it wilts, about 2 minutes. Add the garlic and sauté until fragrant, about 1 minute. Stir in the tomatoes with their juices, wine, and red pepper flakes. Bring to a simmer. Cover and simmer until the tomatoes begin to break down and the chard is very tender, about 5 minutes, stirring occasionally. Season the chard mixture, to taste, with salt and pepper. Meanwhile, bring a large pot of salted water to a boil. Add the angel hair pasta and cook until tender but still firm to the bite, about 6 to 8 minutes, stirring frequently. Drain the angel hair pasta. Add the pasta to the chard mixture and toss to combine. Transfer the pasta to serving bowls. Sprinkle with the olives, cheese, and peppers. Serve immediately.

**Recipe Note:** Add quartered artichokes or sautéed baby bella mushrooms for variety. Also, kale can be used in place of the Swiss chard.

Kimberly Huot
Holcomb Farm CSA
West Granby, Connecticut

65106-05

# BUDÍN DE ACELGA
## (Swiss Chard Casserole)

5 slices bread, crumbled
milk, enough to soak bread
olive oil, for frying vegetables
1 onion, diced
2 cloves garlic, crushed

2 carrots, shredded
1 large bunch of Swiss chard,
  chopped finely
salt and pepper, to taste
1 egg, beaten

Soak bread in milk in large bowl. Set aside. Fry together in large pan: onion, garlic and carrots. Add Swiss chard with a little water until cooked. Add this mixture to the bread and milk mixture. Add salt and pepper and mix well. Put in greased casserole pan. Brush top with one beaten egg. Bake at 350 degrees until firm.

**Recipe Note:** This recipe comes from my Chilean "mother", Edith Navarrette in Temuco, Chile. Best if served with boiled potatoes with oregano and a fresh sliced tomato salad (tomatoes with oil and salt). Yummy! -Heidi

Heidi Loomis
Village Acres Farm
Mifflintown, Pennsylvania

# STRATA WITH SWISS CHARD

2 T. unsalted butter
1 large onion, diced
5-6 slices prosciutto
2 large bunches fresh spinach
1 bunch red chard
2 T. water or broth
freshly grated nutmeg, to
  taste

salt and pepper, to taste
2 small loaves ciabatta bread
6 oz. coarsely grated Gruyère
1 c. finely grated Parmigiano-
  Reggiano cheese
3-1/2 c. whole milk
12 large eggs
2 T. Dijon mustard

Place unsalted butter in a large Dutch oven, sweat the onions until translucent, but not caramelized. Add the prosciutto, cooking a few minutes longer. Finally, add the spinach and chard, and water or broth and cover, reducing heat to wilt the greens. Season with salt, pepper and nutmeg to taste. Meanwhile, cube the bread into 1 inch pieces. In a 12 inch pan or casserole about 1-1/2 inches tall, start layering the ingredients, starting with the bread. Add a layer of the greens mixture, then a layer of cheese. Next, whisk together the milk, eggs and mustard. Season to taste, adding a bit more nutmeg. Pour the custard over the ingredients in the pan, and press down on everything to help the bread absorb. Important: the strata now needs to rest for eight hours or overnight in the refrigerator. Remove the strata out of the refrigerator about 30 minutes before baking. Bake at 400 degrees for about 45 to 55 minutes until it's puffed, browned and the custard has mostly set. Let it rest for about 10 minutes before cutting.

Cynthia Fisher
Great Country Farms
Bluemont, Virginia

65106-05

# Mary blake's swiss chard

1-½ T. vegetable oil
½ c. finely chopped onion
4 c. bite-sized pieces of Swiss
   chard
1-½ c. cooked red kidney beans
   (cooked from dry; or canned,
   drained)

½ c. sour cream
¼ tsp. salt or to taste
⅛ tsp. pepper

In a large skillet heat the oil on medium-high heat, add the onions, cook, stirring until translucent about 2 minutes. Add the Swiss chard, cook stirring until wilted about 3 minutes. Add the beans, cook, stirring until heated through. Remove from heat, stir in the sour cream, salt and pepper.

Mary Blake
Many Hands Organic Farm
Barre, Massachusetts


# Turnip greens
## (Full of antioxidants and fiber)

½ lb. fresh turnip greens
4 c. water
2 slices bacon, chopped

1 small yellow onion, minced
salt and ground black pepper
   to taste

In a 3-quart saucepan, bring the water to a boil. Add the greens and boil for 5 minutes. Drain, squeeze out excess water, and set aside. Put the bacon and onion in a large skillet. Stirring constantly, over medium-low heat until the onion turns translucent and the bacon is slightly crisp, about 6 minutes. Add the greens. Still stirring, cook for about 5 minutes more or until tender and wilted. Salt and pepper to taste. Serves 4.

Les Snyder and Monica Helsley
Sunshine Farm
Lagrange, Kentucky

# PIZZA-STYLE GREENS
## (One pie pan feeds two hungry farmers!)

1 onion, sliced
1 T. olive oil
1-2 garlic cloves, chopped
1 lb. cooking greens, such as
   kale or collards, chopped into
   bite-size pieces and still wet
   from washing

1 c. pizza sauce
mozzarella cheese, shredded or
   grated

Sauté the onions and garlic in oil until brown (the garlic cooks quicker, so you may want to add it when the onions are almost done). Add the wet greens to your pan and cover it with a tight lid. Let the greens steam a few minutes until they are bright green and a little tender, but not so long that they turn a dull green-brown. Loosely fill a pie pan with the greens, onions and garlic until flush, and then add the sauce until the greens are mostly submerged. Cover the top with cheese, just as you would a pizza. Cook in a hot oven until the cheese is melted and brown (about 10 minutes).

**Recipe Note:** Many of our customers have a southern background, so we grow lots of kale and collards for them. My husband, a pizza-lover, created this recipe to help him incorporate this unfamiliar treat into his diet. It's a bit sloppy to serve, but delicious! -Carrie

Carrie & Robert Vaughn
Clagett Farm CSA
Upper Marlboro, Maryland

65106-05

# BAKED RISOTTO WITH GREENS

1 T. olive oil
1 c. finely chopped onion
1 c. uncooked Arborio rice
8 c. greens, chard, spinach,
   kale, etc.
2 c. broth, vegetable or chicken
   based

¼ tsp. salt
¼ tsp. nutmeg
½ c. grated fresh pecorino or
   Parmesan (use more if you
   love cheese)
1-½ c. sliced asparagus

In a Dutch oven sauté onions with rice. Once onions are clear, add greens, broth, salt and nutmeg. Stir these ingredients together and simmer for 5 to 7 minutes. Stir in cheese. Cover and bake for 400 degrees for 30 to 40 minutes.

Elaine Granata
Granata Farms
Denver, Colorado

# Green Pie

7 eggs
8 oz. feta cheese, crumbled
1 onion chopped and sautéed
  or green onions, chopped
1 T. dried oregano or ¼ to ½
  cup chopped fresh oregano
1 tsp. salt

1-2 c. cooked brown rice, wild
  rice or finely chopped nuts
4-6 c. finely shredded greens
¼ c. butter and a small
  amount of olive oil or all olive
  oil
filo dough

Mix together eggs, cheese, onion, oregano. salt, and rice. Then add greens and mix well. In a small bowl, melt ¼ cup butter and mix in some olive oil or substitute butter with all olive oil. Use 20 sheets of dough (see note). Once the dough is open, work fast and keep unused sheets covered with plastic or a towel to keep them from drying out. Half the sheets will go on the bottom, the filling will be spread and the remaining sheets will go on the top. Put 3 to 4 sheets at a time in a greased 9 x 13 pan and brush them with the butter/oil mix or spray them with olive oil. It is important to oil the edges of the sheets to keep them from drying. Spread filling and put another 3 to 4 sheets on top, brushing with the butter/oil mix. Bake at 375 degrees for 50 minutes. Put a sheet of foil loosely on top to keep the top from getting too brown, remove it the last 5 to 10 minutes of baking. Let cool 10 minutes before cutting. To reheat, I put a slice in the toaster oven with foil loosely on top and cook at about 400 degrees for 10 to 15 minutes or until it smells good. This will crisp up the filo again.

**Recipe Note:** Filo dough: Use half a package of filo dough. If it comes in sheets 8½ inches x 13 inches there are usually two packages. If the dough measures 13 inches x 17 inches, cut the dough in half to 8-½ inches x 13 inches and rewrap and seal one half. This yields about 20 sheets of dough.

Patricia Carpenter
Eatwell Farm
Dixon, California

65106-05

# A SIDE OF MIXED GREENS

2 bunches greens, stems
  removed (and center rib for
  kale), sliced in thin ribbons
1-2 T. olive oil

6 or more garlic cloves, minced
salt and pepper, to taste
2 T. balsamic or red wine
  vinegar

Heat oil in a wok or skillet on high heat until fragrant. Add garlic and stir once. Add greens and stir several minutes, until wilted. Lightly salt and pepper and stir in vinegar. Serves 4.

Tom McElderry
Eatwell Farm
Dixon, California

# GREENS WITH THE MAGIC THREE

1 bunch of collards, kale or
  broccoli
¼ c. mirin (a Japanese sweet
  cooking "wine", although it
  has no alcohol)

tamari (natural soy sauce), to
  taste
toasted sesame seed oil

Wash and chop vegetables. Cook in ¼ cup of mirin, although more can be used for taste. Sprinkle with tamari to taste. Cook until just tender, remove from heat and sprinkle and toss with toasted sesame oil.

Amie Hamlin
Hamlet Organic Garden in Brookhaven Hamlet
Long Island, New York

*"You don't have to cook fancy or complicated masterpieces - just good food from fresh ingredients."*

*Julia Child*

# CHEESY GREENS
## (The best-ever kid approved greens recipe!)

3 T. olive oil
1 large bunch of spinach, kale, mustard or chard, washed well
1 large onion, chopped
2 cloves of garlic, minced

2 c. cooked rice
½ c. grated cheese (or more)
soy sauce, to taste
1 cup of cooked kidney, pinto or black beans, optional

Separate greens stems from leaves and chop both into bite-size pieces. (Kale stems may be too tough and may be discarded.) Sauté stems, onion, and garlic in olive oil until onions are tender. Stir in the cooked rice. Place chopped greens on top of rice. Cover pan and cook over low heat until leaves are wilted, but bright green. Add cheese, soy sauce and beans, if desired. Stir until cheese is melted. Serves 4 as a main dish.

Margie Paskert
Barklee Farms
Sagle, Idaho


# GREENS WITH BALSAMIC VINEGAR AND GARLIC

2 tsp. olive oil
1 bunch collards, kale or broccoli
¼ c. balsamic vinegar, or to taste

2-3 garlic cloves, pressed through garlic press

Wash and chop vegetables. Sauté in olive oil over medium heat. Sprinkle with balsamic vinegar to taste, while cooking. When vegetables are cooked to your liking, press garlic on top and mix.

**Recipe Note:** You may prefer to sauté the garlic, although I like keeping it raw for its full health benefits! -Amie

Amie Hamlin
Hamlet Organic Garden in Brookhaven Hamlet
Long Island, New York

65106-05

# SPRING GREENS CHEDDAR QUICHE

1 c. yogurt or sour cream
3 eggs, beaten
3 c. grated sharp cheddar
  cheese
1/2 tsp. basil
dash of salt and pepper

6 scallions (or wild leeks, also
  called ramps)
3 c. chopped spring greens
dash of cayenne pepper
1 unbaked 10 inch pie shell

Mix yogurt, eggs, and cheese. Stir in herbs, spices and scallions. Set aside. Spread greens on bottom of pie shell, then pour egg mixture over top and spread evenly. Add a dash of cayenne pepper to the top. Protect edges of crust from burning with foil rim. Bake at 375 degrees for 45 minutes, until golden and puffy. Let cool for 15 minutes and serve.

Andrea Scott
Merck Forest & Farmland Center CSA
Rupert, Vermont

# SOUTHERN GREENS

1 onion, chopped
2 garlic cloves, minced
1 tomato, chopped
1-2 T. olive oil
1 bunch chard, chopped
1 bunch spinach, cleaned and
  trimmed

1 bunch collards, chopped
1 bunch kale or mustard
  greens, chopped
1 tsp. salt
3 T. Worcestershire sauce
Tabasco, to taste

Sauté the onion, garlic, and tomato in oil until soft. Add all other ingredients and cook until greens are soft.

Sam Hammer
Holcomb Farm CSA
West Granby, Connecticut

# Smoky braised greens

1 tsp. olive oil
1 small onion, cut into ⅛ inch
   wide pieces
2 pieces of bacon, cut into ½
   inch wide strips

1 small bunch of collards
1 small bunch of kale
salt and pepper
braising liquid: beer, water or
   broth

In a large skillet or pot over medium heat, heat the oil and add the onions and bacon. Cook until bacon is crispy and onions brown, about 10 minutes. While the bacon is cooking, wash the greens and cut into 1-inch wide ribbons. Once done, remove bacon and onions from the pan and add the kale and collards, in stages if your pot isn't quite big enough. Sauté until they begin to color up to a vibrant green. Once the greens change color, add the bacon and onion mixture back to the pot, pouring in enough braising liquid (beer option is highly recommended) to cover the bottom of the pan generously so as to get the greens juicy. Cover and turn heat to low, simmering for 20 minutes, keeping an eye on the liquid level, adding more if needed. Season with salt and pepper to taste. If the greens are pretty soupy with braising liquid after the 20 minutes, remove the lid and let the liquid cook off a bit and serve. Serves 2 as a side dish.

Dave Kneeburg
Fairview Gardens
Goleta, California

65106-05

# Five-Grain Salad

6 c. mixed grains (wheat
  berries, hard-wheat berries,
  buckwheat)
1 c. julienned fresh spinach
1 c. julienned arugula
1/2 c. diced red onion

1-1/2 c. Garlic Fennel Vinaigrette
  (recipe follows)
1 head red-leaf lettuce
3-4 Roma tomatoes sliced
3 oz. feta cheese, crumpled
  (optional)

Bring large pot of water to boil and add mixed grains (add longer-cooking grains first). Lower heat and simmer 20 to 30 minutes or until grains are just "al dente." Drain and rinse with cold running water. Drain again and chill. When grains are cold, combine with spinach, arugula, onion, and Garlic Fennel Vinaigrette. Season to taste. Use a large platter and line the outside with the red leaf lettuce. Place the salad mixture on the leaves with the outer part of the leaves exposed. Slice the tomatoes and place at the edge of the salad mixture around the platter next to the lettuce. Sprinkle the salad with feta cheese. Makes 6 to 8 servings.

### Garlic Fennel Vinaigrette

1 c. olive oil
1/2 c. Champagne vinegar or
  other flavored vinegar
1/4 c. minced fresh fennel
2 tsp. fennel seeds
1 T. minced fresh garlic

1/2 tsp. crushed red pepper
1 tsp. oregano
1 tsp. basil
2 tsp. coarsely ground black
  pepper
1 T. salt

Whisk all ingredients together. Place dressing in glass container, cover tightly and let sit overnight to develop flavors.

Richard Jensen
Flying J Farm
Johnstown, Ohio

# STRAWBERRY-MANDARIN SALAD
## (What a delicious summer treat!)

8 c. mesclun greens
2 c. sliced strawberries
1 (11-oz.) can mandarin oranges,
  drained

1 medium sweet onion, sliced
  into rings
1/3 c. sliced almonds, toasted

Combine in a large bowl.

### Dressing

1/4 c. sugar
2 T. cider vinegar
2 T. honey
1-1/4 tsp. lemon juice

1/2 tsp. paprika
1/2 tsp. ground mustard seed
1/2 tsp. grated onion
dash of salt

Stir until combined and cool in refrigerator.

**1/3 c. vegetable oil**

Whisk vegetable oil into refrigerator mix and drizzle over salad mix. Does not refrigerate well after dressed.

Sarah Wu-Norman
Merck Forest & Farmland Center CSA
Rupert, Vermont

65106-05

# Soup of springtime salad greens

1 onion, chopped
3 T. butter
2 c. water
2 c. snap peas
1 c. white wine
bundle of spring herbs (any
    combination of parsley,
    chives, tarragon, thyme,
    chervil)

2 heads of lettuce, chopped
large handful arugula, chopped
salt and pepper, to taste
1 c. cream plus $\frac{1}{2}$ cup (to be
    whipped for garnish)
$\frac{1}{2}$ c. chopped sorrel

Sweat onions in butter over medium-low heat for about 10 minutes in a large soup pot. Blanch snap peas in boiling water for 1 minute and plunge into ice cold water. Reserve pea water. Add wine, pea water, and bundle of herbs to the pot and bring to a boil. Reduce heat and add 1 cup of cream. Simmer for about 10 minutes. Add lettuce and wilt, 2 to 3 minutes. Remove herb bundle and blend soup in small batches in blender until smooth. Add salt and pepper to taste. Garnish with unsweetened whipped cream, chopped sorrel and the peas. Can be served hot or cold. Serves 6.

Lisa Jessup
Common Ground Farm
Beacon, New York

**Recipe Favorites**

65106-05

# HERBS & SEASONING VEGETABLES

# HERBS AND SEASONING VEGETABLES

## Basic pesto

### (Great with tortilla chips or warm pasta!)

3 c. packed fresh basil
1/4 c. fresh parsley
several large garlic cloves
1/3 c. pine nuts

1/3 c. olive oil
1/3 c. fresh Parmesan cheese
salt and pepper

Chop basil, parsley and garlic in food processor. Add the pine nuts, then the olive oil. Stir in the cheese. Season with salt and pepper if desired. Refrigerate.

**Recipe Note:** We love the taste of fresh sweet Genovese basil. Using all or part of Thai basil is also a great variation. -Shelley and Mike

Shelley Squier & Mike Donnelly
Squier Squash & Donnelly Farms
North English, Iowa

# WANDA COIL'S FABULOUS PESTO
## (Delicious pesto that led to a marriage proposal!)

2 c. firmly packed fresh basil
3/4 c. grated Parmesan or
  Romano cheese
1/4 c. pine nuts

4 garlic cloves, roughly chopped
1/2 c. olive oil (use more if
  necessary)

Combine basil, cheese, pine nuts and garlic in food processor or blender. With machine running, add the oil slowly in a stream. Freeze in ice cube trays. When frozen, remove cubes and put in a freezer bag for storage.

**Recipe Note:** In 1999, Keith had an organic farm in Wooster, Ohio. I loved his large leaf basil and enjoyed making huge batches of pesto. In a weak moment he told me he would marry me for my pesto. In 2000, he moved to Virginia, and we were married in 2004, and have a farm in Nellysford, Virginia where we grow lots of garlic and basil! - Beverly

Keith Dix & Beverly Lacey
Blue Heron Farm
Nellysford, Virginia

# PESTO EGG SALAD SANDWICHES

6 hard-boiled eggs
1/4 c. pesto
1/2 tsp. Dijon mustard

sour cream and/or mayonnaise,
  to taste
salt and pepper, to taste

Mix and serve on your favorite sandwich bread.

Keith Dix & Beverly Lacey
Blue Heron Farm
Nellysford, Virginia

65106-05

# BASIL-ZUCCHINI PASTA SALAD

³/₄ lb. orzo or alphabet pasta
4 medium zucchini
1 tsp. salt
2-¹/₂ c. fresh basil
1 garlic clove

¹/₂ tsp. oregano
1 c. olive oil
¹/₄ c. lemon juice
¹/₄ c. Parmesan cheese

Cook orzo or alphabet pasta in water or seasoned stock. Drain and cool. Grate zucchini into a colander and sprinkle with salt. Let sit for 10 minutes and squeeze dry. In a food processor, blend fresh basil, with garlic, oregano, olive oil, and lemon juice. Mix everything together with Parmesan cheese. Chill.

Anne Morgan
Lakes & Valley CSA/Midheaven Farms
Park Rapids, Minnesota

# SUMMER CHICKEN

1 roasting chicken
1 bunch fresh basil
5-¹/₂ c. chicken broth
1 c. chopped onion
5 parsley sprigs
salt and pepper, to taste

3 T. butter
3 T. flour
¹/₃ c. Dijon mustard
¹/₃ c. cream
2 T. chopped parsley

Stuff chicken with basil and put in a heavy pan. Pour in broth. Bring to a boil and then simmer while adding onion and parsley sprigs, salt, and pepper. Cook for 40 minutes or until done. Remove chicken from broth and keep warm. To make the sauce to spoon over chicken: measure out 2 cups of broth in a separate pan and bring to a boil. In another pan melt butter, add flour, and cook without browning for about 5 minutes. Remove from heat and pour in the boiling chicken broth. Whisk the sauce as it bubbles and then return to a low heat. Bring to a boil and cook for 5 minutes. Remove basil from chicken. Whisk the basil, mustard and cream into the sauce. Remove from heat and cover. Carve chicken and arrange on a platter. Spoon sauce over chicken and serve hot.

Rusty & Claire Orner
Quiet Creek Herb Farm
Brookville, Pennsylvania

# TARRAGON CHICKEN WITH FORTY CLOVES OF GARLIC

1 roasting chicken
1 bunch tarragon
1 apple
40 cloves of garlic
2-1/2 c. chicken broth
1 c. chopped onion
5 parsley sprigs

salt and pepper, to taste
3 T. butter
3 T. flour
1/3 c. Dijon mustard
1/3 c. cream
2 T. chopped parsley

Stuff chicken with tarragon, apple and 6 cloves of garlic and put in heavy pan. Arrange remaining garlic around the chicken. Cook for 1 to 2 hours or until done. Remove from heat and keep warm. Pour broth into saucepan. Bring to a boil and then simmer adding onion, parsley sprigs, and salt/pepper. In another pan melt butter add flour. Cook without browning for about 5 minutes. Remove from heat and pour in the boiling chicken broth. Whisk the sauce as it bubbles and then return to a low heat. Bring to a boil and cook for 5 minutes. Remove tarragon from chicken. Whisk the tarragon, mustard and cream into the sauce. Remove from heat and cover. Carve chicken and arrange on a platter. Spoon sauce over chicken and serve hot sprinkled with chopped parsley.

Rusty & Claire Orner
Quiet Creek Herb Farm
Brookville, Pennsylvania

*"I feel a recipe is only a theme, which an intelligent cook can play each time with a variation."*

Madam Benoit

65106-05

# QUIET CREEK'S CHICKEN SALAD

4 lbs. chicken breast (organic, free range)
4 oz. fresh tarragon
2 stalks of celery plus 1-½ pounds of celery, diced
1 large onion plus 1 tablespoon of onion, minced

1 T. salt
½ tsp. white pepper
2 c. mayonnaise
2 tsp. lemon juice
20 oz. diced pineapple

Boil chicken for 45 minutes with 4 ounces of fresh tarragon, 2 stalks of celery, and one large onion. Drain. Cube chicken and combine all remaining ingredients except pineapple. Chill and add pineapple before serving.

Rusty & Claire Orner
Quiet Creek Herb Farm
Brookville, Pennsylvania


# SUMMER GREENS OMELETTE

1 bunch of onions, chard, parsley, cilantro, basil, or any combination of these, finely chopped

2 T. butter or olive oil
eggs
yogurt, kefir, or sour cream
cheese, such as cheddar

Sauté the onions in butter or oil on medium heat for 2 to 3 minutes, until slightly browned. Add chard and lower the heat, sauté 2 to 3 more minutes. If not using chard, add the other greens, and mix with the onions, so everything is evenly heated. Beat eggs well (using 2 eggs per person), with yogurt (1 to 2 tablespoons per person), season with salt and pepper to taste. Pour the egg mixture on top of the greens in the frying pan, beat while pouring. Fry on medium-high heat, until omelette can be flipped. If it's too thick or runny, use spatula to scrape the cooked part into the middle, so the uncooked parts can run out. Omelette will be slightly broken-up. Serve with toast or eat plain, sprinkled with cheese.

Esther Mandelheim & Pablo Elliott
Stoney Lonesome Farm
Gainesville, Virginia

# SWEET CORN WITH THYME

6 ears sweet corn, with husks
1-2 tsp. extra-virgin olive oil, per
cob

2 T. fresh thyme

Peel back corn husks and remove the silks. Drizzle olive oil over corn and sprinkle with thyme. Smooth the husks back in place. Place on a preheated barbecue and cook for 20 to 30 minutes, turning frequently. Serve hot.

**Recipe Note:** This is a great option if your picnic plans include a grill. If not, roast corn ahead of time in the oven and serve at room temperature.

Karen Vollmecke
Vollmecke Orchards CSA
West Brandywine, Pennsylvania


# PASTA FAGOLI

## (Italian soul food; ready in less than 20 minutes!)

3 T. extra virgin olive oil
1 onion, chopped
3 celery stalks, chopped
3 carrots, chopped
3 garlic cloves, minced
fresh rosemary
fresh thyme
1 (8-oz.) can tomato sauce

2 c. vegetable stock
4 c. water
3-4 c. cannellini beans, fully
  cooked
1-3/4 c. uncooked dinatale
  pasta
1/2 c. Parmigiano Reggiano
  cheese

Heat oil in a large soup pot, add onions, celery and carrots and sauté for 3 to 5 minutes. Add garlic, sauté 1 to 2 minutes. Add rosemary and thyme, sauté one minute more. Add tomato sauce, vegetable stock and water; cover and heat to a boil. Once boiling, add beans and pasta, simmer uncovered at medium heat until pasta is fully cooked. Serve in bowls sprinkled with grated cheese.

**Recipe Note:** The fragrant smell and delicious taste of the rosemary and thyme make this soup worth every bite!

Julie Sochacki

65106-05

# DEB'S PULLED PORK ROAST

1 pork shoulder or butt roast     1 jar of your favorite mustard

Dry Rub: one tablespoon each of seasoned salt, chili powder, paprika, ground black pepper, garlic powder, turmeric, onion powder, cumin, and 1 to 2 dried ancho chilies ground in a food processor.

Combine dry rub ingredients in bowl. Cover all sides of roast with mustard and then cover with dry rub. Wrap roast in foil and cook in preheated oven at 300 degrees until roast is done (about 170 degrees) and meat is falling off the bone. Remove from oven and let stand for 20 minutes. Pull meat off bone serve on a plate with BBQ sauce or as a sandwich.

Debra Fuller
Merck Forest & Farmland Center CSA
Rupert, Vermont


# CHICKEN STOCK
## (Excellent immune system booster!)

2-3 qts. water
chicken giblets and carcass
2 celery stalks
1-2 onions, remove skin and
   quarter

3 carrots
garlic, peeled and chopped
peppercorns
4-5 bay leaves
thyme

In 2 to 3 quarts of water, boil giblets and carcass of a chicken with 2 stalks celery, 1 to 2 onions and carrots. Add garlic, $\frac{1}{2}$ to 1 teaspoon of sea salt per quart water, peppercorns, 4 to 5 bay leaves and thyme. Bring to a boil then simmer for several hours. Strain, place in quart containers and freeze. As the stock cools it will gel, this is the sign of a good chicken stock. The fat will rise to the top and can be easily scraped off.

**Recipe Note:** When you are feeling sick in the winter, pull a quart out of the freezer and make a simple soup. Sure beats bullion cubes!

Dave Chirico & Matt Ferut
Two Guys Farm
Reynoldsville, Pennsylvania

# BOMBAY CHICKEN

½ c. bread crumbs
½ tsp. oregano
½ tsp. turmeric
⅔ tsp. sea salt
½ tsp. chili powder

½ tsp. parsley
2 chicken breasts, cleaned and
    dried
olive oil, to coat chicken and
    pan

Mix all ingredients in a plastic bag except chicken and oil. Lightly coat chicken with oil and place in the bag. Shake bag to coat chicken with crumb mixture. Place chicken in an uncovered, greased glass baking dish. Bake at 375 degrees for about 45 to 55 minutes.

Nedra Hawkins
J.L. Hawkins Family Farm
North Manchester, Indiana


**Recipe Favorites**

65106-05

# PEAS & BEANS

# PEAS & BEANS

## TIPS FOR COOKING BEANS

The preparation involved before cooking beans is really important in order to receive all the nutrients beans have to offer.

Sort (pick out any deformed or broken beans). Wash and soak at least overnight. Pour off soaking water (adzuki beans are the exception) to remove phytic acid which interferes with digestion. Rinse again after soaking. Skim off foam during the first half hour of boiling. Use a heavy bottom pot. Cook with a 2 inch piece of kombu seaweed in the bottom of the pot. It will help to soften the beans. Keep an eye on the water level. The beans need to have water covering them most of the cooking time. Add salt when beans are about $1/2$ hour away from "finished", or in other words, when they are about 80% cooked. They will absorb the salt better when soft. If the salt is present from the start, they may remain hard.

Annie Sheble
St. Martin de Tours Organic Farm
Palermo, Maine

# MAINE BEANS AND CARROTS

2 c. dry beans: (Yellow Eye, Jacob's Cattle, Soldier, Red Kidney, Marfax, to name a few favorites)
1-2 pieces kombu, soaked for 10 minutes and diced (optional)
½ c. diced celery
1 c. diced onion
½ c. diced carrot
1 T. barley miso, or shoyu, or sea salt, to taste

Wash and soak beans for 6 to 8 hours. Discard soaking water. Place kombu and beans into heavy pot. Add just enough water to cover. Bring to a boil without a cover, skimming off any foam. Reduce heat and simmer 10 minutes. Cover pot and cook for 1-½ to 2 hours until 80% done, adding water as needed to make sure beans stay covered. Add celery, onion, carrot and seasoning. Cook for another ½ hour or until tender. Remove from heat and place in serving bowl.

Annie Sheble
St. Martin de Tours Organic Farm
Palermo, Maine

# WHITE BEANS WITH HERBED ONION-GARLIC CONFIT

4 qts. water
1-¼ c. dried white beans
1 small bundle of English thyme
3 T. olive oil
1 large onion, finely chopped
6 garlic cloves, finely chopped
2 c. chicken broth
1 T. chopped fresh rosemary
1 T. chopped fresh winter savory

Place beans in 2 quarts of water, bring to boil and let them soak for one hour. Drain beans and rinse under cold water. Add 2 quarts of cold water and add thyme, boil gently for 30 to 60 minutes or until tender. While beans are cooking, heat olive oil in a saucepan over medium heat. Add onion and garlic, stirring often for 8 minutes. Pour stock into garlic mixture and add remaining herbs. Boil for about 30 minutes. Drain beans and add to garlic mixture for 5 minutes. Season with salt and pepper.

Rusty & Clare Orner
Quiet Creek Herb Farm
Brookville, Pennsylvania

65106-05

# SWEET-AND-SPICY BARBECUED BEANS WITH KALE

## (Compliments of member Martha Kaiser)

olive oil, for sautéing onions
1 c. chopped onions
4 garlic cloves, minced
pinch of red pepper flakes
8 c. chopped kale or collards
 (about ³/₄ pound)
1 (15-oz.) can tomato sauce
2 tsp. chili powder

2 T. brown sugar
1 T. soy sauce
pepper and additional crushed
 garlic to taste
2 T. Dijon mustard
1 T. cider vinegar
2 (16-oz.) cans kidney beans,
 rinsed and drained

Heat oil in large skillet over medium heat. Add onion, garlic and red pepper flakes. Sauté about 5 minutes. Add kale or collards and stir fry until wilted. (Depending upon the tenderness of greens, it is recommended to add a few tablespoons of water to cover and steam the greens a bit before proceeding.) Combine and add remaining ingredients, cover, and cook until done, stirring often to keep from sticking to the skillet.

**Recipe Note:** Great served with brown rice or organic potatoes.

Anja Mast & Michael VanderBrug
Trillium Haven Farm CSA
Jenison, Michgan

# SATURDAY NIGHT YELLOW EYES WITH MAINE MAPLE SYRUP

Dried beans, as early Americans understood, are storehouses of nutrients, being rich in vitamin A and potassium, and also containing vitamins C, B1 and 2, calcium, phosphorus, protein, and a bit of iron. Baked Beans, so common on Saturday nights all over New England, continue to please and satisfy. This version is made with handsome Yellow Eyes and Maine Maple Syrup.

3 c. Yellow Eye dried beans
1 medium-sized onion, sliced thin
2 medium-sized, tart winter apples, cored and sliced thin OR a handful of dried apple slices

plenty of freshly ground black pepper
1 heaping tsp. dried mustard
1 heaping tsp. powdered ginger
1/2 c. maple syrup
enough water to barely cover

On Friday night pick over carefully, removing any stones from beans. Rinse, then soak overnight in a big bowl with about 3 times as much water. On Saturday morning, discard water, then place hydrated beans into a big pot with just enough fresh water to barely cover. Bring to a boil. Lower heat and simmer until skins begin to peel when you blow on them. When ready, drain, and pour them into a large, ceramic bean pot. Add remaining ingredients. Place in a 300 degree oven and bake all day, adding hot water as necessary to keep the beans covered but not swimming.

**Recipe Note:** Do not add salt to the beans, because it toughens the skins. Salt if desired after beans are cooked. Also, yellow eyes cook much faster than red kidney beans, for instance. I've managed to produce good results with only a four-hour baking at 340 degrees. - Jean Ann

Jean Ann Pollard
The Simply Grande Gardens
Winslow, Maine

65106-05

# BEAN SALAD

1 'Suyo long' cucumber or 2
  'Supersett' cucumbers,
  quartered, seeded and sliced
  ¼ inch thick
salt and pepper
2 c. green, purple or wax beans,
  ends removed and sliced
½ bag frozen shelled Edamame
  (edible soy beans), rinsed
  (optional)

1 can Cannellini (Garbanzo/
  Chick Pea, Kidney or Black
  Beans), rinsed
1 small onion, thinly sliced
3 garlic cloves, minced
2 T. wine vinegar
1 (15-oz.) jar quartered
  marinated artichoke hearts
  including liquid

## Optional Additions

3 T. finely sliced fresh herbs
2 thinly sliced carrots

2 celery ribs, sliced
1 can ripe olives

Place cucumber in bowl, sprinkle with salt and allow to sit at room temperature for 15 to 30 minutes. Rinse well. Cover fresh beans and Edamame with water plus 1 teaspoon salt in a microwave safe dish, cook on high for 4 to 5 minutes (cook longer if you do not like crunchy beans). Rinse with cold water. In a separate bowl mix garlic, onion, wine vinegar and artichokes. Add all vegetables to dressing, toss and season with salt and pepper to taste. Refrigerate for a few hours to allow flavors to develop. Can be refrigerated overnight.

Amy Nichols, Clemson University
Calhoun Field Laboratory Student Organic Farm
Clemson, South Carolina

# THREE BEAN SALAD

3 cans beans, different colors, drained
1 sweet onion, chopped
1 green pepper, chopped (or ripened red or yellow pepper)

½ c. oil
½ c. sugar
½ c. vinegar
1 tsp. salt

Mix and refrigerate. If eaten immediately, the sugar and salt are still a bit crunchy. The flavors are not melded but separate. However, it does keep well in the refrigerator for a week or more.

Harriet Kattenberg
Seedtime & Harvest
Hull, Iowa

# SNAP BEAN AND CHERRY TOMATO PASTA SALAD

¾ lb. bow tie pasta
¾ lb. small green and/or purple snap beans
⅔ c. olive oil
¼ c. red wine vinegar
1 large garlic clove, minced or pressed
1 tsp. Dijon/brown mustard

salt and pepper
2 c. cherry tomatoes
3 T. chopped basil leaves
2 T. chopped fresh chives
2 T. chopped fresh oregano leaves
1 c. crumbled feta cheese

Cook the pasta according to the package directions. Blanch the beans until just tender (or add them to the pasta fresh). Mix the oil, vinegar, garlic, mustard, and salt and pepper to make the dressing. Add the tomatoes, herbs, cheese and dressing to the pasta and beans, and serve. Serves 8 to 10 as a side dish.

Evan & Jodi Verbanic
Cherry Valley Community Farm
Cherry Valley, Pennsylvania

65106-05

# BUSH BEANS WITH TARRAGON

(Fresh tarragon adds a great flavor to these beans.)

1-1/2 T. salt
1 lb. fresh beans
3-4 T. olive oil
1 shallot, finely diced
1 sprig fresh tarragon, finely chopped

salt and pepper to taste
2 T. tarragon vinegar or cider vinegar

Add salt and beans to 4 quarts of boiling water. Cook beans until tender, but still firm. Remove beans from the pot and set them on a kitchen towel to dry for a few minutes. Transfer them to a bowl and toss them with olive oil, shallot, tarragon, and salt and pepper. Sprinkle on vinegar immediately before serving.

Franz Rulofson, College of the Redwoods
Sustainable Agriculture Farm
Shively, California

*"A good cook is like a sorceress who dispenses happiness."*

*Elsa Schiaparelli*

# THE BEST GREEN BEAN SALAD
## (Compliments of member Laurel Graney)

| | |
|---|---|
| 1-1/2 lbs. fresh green beans | 1 c. crumbled feta cheese |
| 1 c. diced red onion | 1 c. toasted walnut pieces |

Snap beans into pieces, boil for 4 minutes and plunge into cold water. Drain and set aside.

### Dressing

| | |
|---|---|
| 3/4 c. olive oil | 1 tsp. salt |
| 1/4 c. white wine vinegar | 1/2 tsp. diced fresh garlic |
| 1/2 c. finely chopped packed basil | freshly black ground pepper |

Combine oil, vinegar, basil, salt, garlic and pepper. Shake and refrigerate. Keep all ingredients separate. Just prior to serving, toss beans, onions, cheese, and walnuts with dressing.

**Recipe Note:** Laurel has adorned our potluck table with this outstanding salad on several occasions. She always has a handful of the recipes printed out because folks want to know how to have a repeat performance! -Elizabeth

Elizabeth Keen
Indian Line Farm
South Egremont, Massachusetts


# GREEN BEANS AND GARLIC
## (Simple and delicious!)

| | |
|---|---|
| 2 c. green beans cut into 2 inch pieces | 2 cloves garlic, minced |
| olive oil | salt, to taste |

Sauté green beans in olive oil with cover on, stirring as needed. When almost tender, add garlic. Cook 1 minute more.

Tracie Smith
Tracie's Farm CSA
Sullivan, New Hampshire

65106-05

# GREEN BEAN AND FINGERLING POTATO SALAD

## (Make this and watch it disappear!)

2 lbs. fingerling potatoes
1 lb. green beans
1/4 c. in-season fresh herbs

2 T. olive oil
1/3 tsp. lemon zest

Boil potatoes in salted water for about 10 minutes. Drain. Boil beans in salted water for 4 minutes or until tender-crisp. Drain. In a large bowl, toss everything together. Salad can be made a day ahead of time. Serve at room temperature.

Shelley Squier & Mike Donnelly
Squier Squash & Donnelly Farms
North English, Iowa


# GREEN BEAN TOMATO CURRY

1 T. olive or vegetable oil
1 T. fresh minced ginger
1 T. cumin seeds
3/4 tsp. brown mustard seeds
2 chopped tomatoes
1 tsp. turmeric

3 c. chopped green beans
salt, to taste
a dash of cayenne pepper
  (optional)
Thai basil or cilantro

Heat oil in a pot. Add fresh ginger, cumin seeds and brown mustard seeds and sauté over medium heat until the mustard seeds pop, but don't burn. Add chopped tomatoes and sauté for a few minutes, stirring frequently, until they become mushy. Stir in turmeric, chopped green beans, salt to taste, and cayenne if desired, and simmer until beans are tender, about 15 minutes. Adjust salt and add Thai basil and/or cilantro. Serve over rice.

Tracie Smith
Tracie's Farm CSA
Sullivan, New Hampshire

# Recipe Favorites

# PEPPERS & EGGPLANT

# PEPPERS & EGGPLANT

## ROASTED PEPPERS

### Roasting the Peppers

**6 large red bell peppers**

To roast and peel peppers, split pepper in half lengthwise, and remove the seeds and core. Place skin side up on a broiler pan and broil until the skin is evenly charred. Transfer from the pan to a paper bag. Close the bag and let steam for 10 to 15 minutes. When the peppers are cool enough to handle, the skin should peel away easily. Peppers can also be roasted on an outdoor grill by placing the peppers skin side down.

### Seasoning the Peppers

| | |
|---|---|
| ½ tsp. crushed oregano | 3 T. balsamic vinegar |
| 1 T. chopped fresh parsley | 2 garlic cloves, minced |
| ¼ c. extra virgin olive oil | salt and pepper to taste |

Slice the peeled roasted peppers and place in a bowl. Add the remaining ingredients and mix. Let marinate in refrigerator for a few hours or over night. Before serving bring to room temperature. Serve with crusty Italian bread.

**Recipe Note:** Roasted peppers are great on sandwiches, salads, pizzas, pasta salads, and omelettes, just to name a few!

Julie Sochacki

# ROASTED RED PEPPER YOGURT DIP

## (Make this dip as hot as you'd like!)

1-1/2 c. roasted red peppers,
  2-3 large
16 oz. low fat, plain yogurt
1/2 c. green chiles, chopped
  (choose your desired level of
  heat)

1 garlic clove, minced
Dippers: vegetables, pita
  wedges or chips

Roast red peppers and drain peppers while cooling. Remove skin, seeds and membranes when cool. Purée peppers in a food processor or blender. Add yogurt, chiles and garlic. Mix until well blended and refrigerate. Serve with assorted dippers of your choice.

**Recipe Note:** The yogurt tends to "cool" the chiles somewhat. Make certain the peppers are drained well of any oil used in the roasting process or the dip will be runny. This dip is a nice way to encourage reluctant children to eat their veggies!

Margaret Pennings
Common Harvest Farms
Osceola, Wisconsin

65106-05

# Stuffed poblano chiles

2-3 medium or large chilies, halved lengthwise and seeded
¾ c. fresh or frozen corn kernels, thawed if frozen
¼ c. chopped red onion
¼ c. chopped red bell pepper
2 T. chopped fresh cilantro

2 oz. sharp cheddar cheese, shredded (¾ cup)
1 fresh jalapeño, seeded and minced
1 T. dried bread crumbs
½ tsp. salt
sour cream

Lightly grease a baking sheet. Arrange the pepper halves on the baking sheet. Combine all the remaining ingredients except the sour cream in a mixing bowl and toss thoroughly. Fill the pepper halves with this mixture. Bake at 375 degrees until the peppers are tender and the filling is heated through, 30 minutes. Serve immediately, topped with a dollop of sour cream.

**Recipe Note:** Poblano peppers are rich in vitamin C. They are excellent roasted, peeled and added to soups, stews and sauces, or halved and stuffed before baking.

Les Snyder & Monica Helsley
Sunshine Farm
Lagrange, Kentucky

# CRAB STUFFED POBLANO PEPPERS
## (Crabmeat makes these peppers special!)

1 lb. fresh lump crabmeat
1/2 c. fat-free sour cream
1/4 c. seasoned dry bread
  crumbs
2 T. roasted red peppers (from
  water-packed jar)

4 poblano peppers, halved and
  seeded
8 tsp. grated Parmesan cheese

Coat a shallow baking pan with cooking spray. In a medium bowl, combine crabmeat, sour cream, bread crumbs and roasted red peppers. Mix gently to combine, being careful not to break up the crab. Spoon crab mixture into halves of poblano peppers and arrange side by side in pan. Top mixture with Parmesan cheese. Cover pan with foil and bake at 275 degrees for 20 minutes. Remove foil and bake 15 minutes more, until peppers are soft and cheese begins to brown.

Les Snyder & Monica Helsley
Sunshine Farm
Lagrange, Kentucky

65106-05

# CHILI RELLANOS CASSEROLE

8-12 green peppers, (Anaheim, poblano, bell peppers and other sweet peppers)
1 yellow onion, diced
olive oil
4 garlic cloves
1/2 tsp. pepper
1 tsp. salt
1 T. cumin
1 T. chili powder
1 c. corn, cut off the cob
4 eggs
1-1/2 c. whole milk
2 T. flour
1 c. shredded sharp cheddar cheese
1 c. shredded jack cheese

Poke several holes in each pepper to allow air to escape while roasting. Place peppers on a cookie sheet. Roast peppers under broiler, turning occasionally (every 5 to 10 minutes) so that the skin on each side is blackened. Remove from oven and place in a paper bag until cool enough to handle. Remove from bag, peel off skin, cut off the top and remove seeds. Slice peppers in long strips. Sauté onion in olive oil until translucent. Add garlic, pepper, salt, cumin, and chili powder. Sauté another 2 to 3 minutes. Remove from heat and stir in the corn. In a bowl, mix together the eggs, milk and flour. In a baking dish (approximately 9 x 9 x 3) layer 1/3 of the peppers, half the corn, 1/3 of the cheese; repeat. Pour the egg mixture over it. Top with the remaining peppers and cheese. Bake at 350 degrees for approximately 45 minutes or until casserole is slightly puffed in the center and golden brown on the edges. Allow to cool for 20 minutes before serving.

**Recipe Note:** This recipe is a great way to use up some of those assorted peppers in the summer. If you like some heat add a jalapeño or a wax pepper to the mix. If you don't like hot foods just use sweet peppers.

Solyssa Visalli
Cop Copi Farms
La Grand, Oregon

# CHILI RELLENOS

4 poblano peppers
1/2 lb. grated Mexican cheeses
white flour

2 eggs
canola oil for frying

Wash the chiles and lay them on a sheet under the broiler to blacken. Turn them until the skin is blistering on all sides. Put them in a sealed container and let them cool briefly. Peel the chiles and gently pull out the stem. If the flesh tears down the side, use this as your seam and finish the cut so the chile lays open in one piece. Have grated cheese ready. Prepare a plate with flour to roll the chiles in. Separate the eggs and beat the whites until stiff. Lightly beat the yolks and then fold them into the whites with just a sprinkling of flour. Keep this mixture chilled. Squeeze a fistful of cheese into a torpedo shape and place it in the center of a chile. Wrap the chile around it. The chiles can be stuffed ahead and frozen. Preheat the oven to 350 degrees. Heat oil at least 2 inches deep in a heavy pot on the stove to 325 degrees or until the surface shimmers and a little egg batter quickly browns. Roll each chile lightly in the flour, brushing off any excess, then dip it into the egg mixture. This is messy. Put it carefully in the hot oil and pour a little more egg mixture on top. Fry only as many chiles at a time that will easily fit. Place chiles on towels to absorb some of the oil, then put them in a baking dish and place them in the oven for about 10 minutes or until the cheeses start to bubble out a little. Serve one chile as an appetizer, two as a main dish.

**Recipe Note:** Homemade chile rellenos are so much better than anything I've ever tasted at a restaurant. I like to serve each chile on a small plate over a bed of green roasted tomatillos salsa on one side and red roasted tomato salsa on the other, with a decadent dollop of cream or sour cream on top! -Tom

Tom McElderry
Eatwell Farm
Dixon, California

65106-05

# Stuffed pepper soup

1 c. chopped onion
¼ c. chopped celery
1 garlic clove, minced
2 c. chopped green bell pepper
2 T. olive oil
½ lb. lean ground beef (or tofu crumble)
¼ c. uncooked white rice
1 (16-oz.) can crushed tomatoes
½ c. tomato juice
3 c. water
2 T. chopped fresh parsley
2 tsp. white sugar
1 tsp. sea salt
1 tsp. ground black pepper
¼ tsp. cinnamon

In a large skillet, sauté onion, celery, garlic and green pepper in olive oil until soft and tender. Do not brown. Stir beef into cooked vegetables. Cook until browned, about 10 minutes. Stir rice into the beef and vegetable mixture. Add tomatoes, juice, water, parsley, sugar, salt and pepper to the mixture. Cover and simmer for 45 minutes or until rice is cooked. Adjust liquid if needed. Stir in cinnamon and salt and pepper to taste. Garnish each serving with a parsley sprig. Serves 6.

Nancy Couch Nowak
Maple Creek Farm
Yale, Michigan

# Pop's peppers and eggs

2-3 garden-fresh medium bell peppers
6 eggs, scrambled
1 T. olive oil

Put 1 tablespoon olive oil in a skillet and heat to medium. De-seed peppers and slice, rinse in cold water, do not pat dry. Add peppers to the skillet and cover. Sauté the peppers for approximately 15 minutes or until tender. Add scrambled eggs and enjoy sandwiched between warm French bread.

**Recipe Note:** We eat this for breakfast or dinner. My dad has fixed this for years. It's so simple, but it's one of my favorites! -Angela

Angela Thiel
St. Fairsted
Woodville, Texas

# EGGPLANT SKILLET
## (Freeze the leftovers!)

1 lb. ground beef
1 garlic clove, chopped
1 large or 2 small eggplant,
  peeled and cubed
1 green sweet pepper or/and
  yellow or red
1 onion, chopped

3 c. peeled and chopped
  tomatoes
3 fresh basil leaves
1 pinch fresh oregano
salt and pepper, to taste
brown or white rice, fully cooked

Brown the ground beef, add garlic, drain off fat. Add the eggplant, cooking for about 10 minutes. Add remaining ingredients, cover and simmer for 15 minutes. Serve over a bed of rice.

**Recipe Note:** This is an excellent vegan dish without the beef. When I make it, I normally triple the recipe and it freezes REALLY well! -Mae

Mae Swindal
Old Maids Farm
Glastonbury, Connecticut


# EASY EGGPLANT

eggplant
Parmesan cheese

mayonnaise
garlic powder (optional)

Peel and slice any variety eggplant into $1/4$-$1/3$ inch slices. (Peeling is unnecessary if it is very fresh or one of the Japanese types.) Lay slices on a greased cookie sheet. Spread each slice with thin layer of mayonnaise, sprinkle generously with Parmesan cheese and a dusting of garlic powder. Bake at 400 degrees for approximately 10 minutes or until fork tender. The cooking time varies with eggplant variety and thickness of slices.

Genevieve Stillman
Stillman's Greenhouses & Farmstand
Lunenburg & New Braintree, Massachusetts

65106-05

# Scalloped Eggplant

1 large or 2 small eggplant
½ tsp. salt
¼ tsp. pepper
2 c. canned tomatoes, well
    drained
½ c. finely chopped onion

green pepper, diced (optional)
2 eggs, well beaten
2 c. cornbread crumbs
milk
grated cheese

Peel, pare and cube the eggplant. Place cubes in pan, cover with water. Boil until tender and drain thoroughly. Add salt and pepper, mash the mixture with a potato masher or fork. Mash the tomatoes with the onion and green peppers. Add to the eggplant along with eggs and cornbread crumbs. Pour into greased casserole and pour in enough milk to cover. Top with grated cheese and bake at 375 degrees for 30 to 45 minutes.

Jolinda Hamilton
Hamilton Farms
Clinton, Arkansas

*"Find something you're passionate about and keep tremendously interested in it."*

*Julia Child*

# EGGPLANT PIZZA

eggplant
large tomatoes or chunky
   sauce

cheese
oil
favorite herbs

Slice eggplant into uniform $1/4$ to $1/2$ inch thick rounds (the skin is healthy too, but you may prefer to peel). Pour a couple of tablespoons of oil on a large cookie sheet and spread to cover. Lightly sprinkle your favorite dry herbs or "salt" blend over oil. Swivel a side of the eggplant over a bit of the oil layer, flip over and position on sheet. Repeat with all, redoing a bit of oil mix if needed. Bake in oven for 10 to 15 minutes. Prick with fork to see when they feel almost tender, then flip over. Top with one $1/8$ to $1/4$ inch thick slice(s) of tomato for quick version, OR sauté a tomato sauce using chopped tomatoes, onions, peppers, garlic, favorite herbs, and spread one to two tablespoons over top of each eggplant round. Sprinkle with as much grated cheese, or slices of cheese as you would like on top of tomato layer and bake for another 10 to 15 minutes.

Jill Fish
Pitcher Mountain CSA
Stoddard, New Hampshire

65106-05

# EGGPLANT CASSEROLE
## (Notice that the eggplant is not fried!)

1 T. olive oil
½ c. flour, seasoned with salt
  and pepper
3 eggs
3-5 eggplant (Asian or Italian),
  sliced ³/₈ inch thick into long
  pieces (or alternatively use
  squash)

several large tomatoes, sliced
  ³/₈ inch thick
1-2 sweet onions, sliced
3-5 garlic cloves, minced
fresh basil or sage, chopped
grated cheese (a combination
  of cheddar and Parmesan)
1 c. milk

Spread oil on bottom of an oven-proof casserole dish. Beat an egg (or use water or milk instead of an egg). Dip the eggplant and/or squash slices in the egg, then in the flour. Spread evenly over the bottom of the casserole dish. Layer onions, tomatoes, garlic, basil or sage, and cheese in any order preferred. Reserve some cheese and sprinkle over the top of the casserole. For a one dish meal, beat the remaining two eggs and add the milk. Pour into casserole. Bake uncovered at 375 degrees for 35 to 45 minutes or until cheese is browned, eggplant is tender, and custard is set.

**Recipe Note:** Zucchini or other summer squash can be used instead of or along with the eggplant. If you choose not to add the eggs and the milk, you can include a layer of sliced potatoes for a heartier dish.

Margie Paskert
Barklee Farms
Sagle, Idaho

# GRILLED EGGPLANT

## (Squash can be substituted for eggplant.)

Eggplant, zucchini or other
  summer squash
balsamic vinegar

olive oil
salt

Brush vegetable slices with balsamic vinegar and let them rest on a plate for at least 5 minutes. Brush lightly with olive oil just before placing on the grill, over direct heat. Grill, turning once, until they soften somewhat, about 10 to 15 minutes. Salt to taste and serve immediately.

Jeanne Duffner
Barklee Farm
Sagle, Idaho

65106-05

# SICILIAN EGGPLANT
## (Stuffed with garlic and cheese)

1 large eggplant or 2 medium
  to small eggplants
2 T. olive oil
1 onion, finely chopped
8 cloves garlic, sliced
1 lb. tomatoes, chopped
1/4 tsp. crushed red pepper

sugar
salt and pepper, to taste
(5-oz.) aged provolone cheese,
  sliced
bunches of fresh mint, basil
  and parsley

Cut off the stem of the eggplant and roll on the counter to soften. Let sit in a bowl with salt water for 1 hour. Make slits lengthwise, spaced 1 inch apart, 1/2 inch deep, staying away from the ends. Be sure not to cut the eggplant in pieces. It should remain whole, just creating enough space to fill with cheese and garlic. Meanwhile, heat olive oil in a casserole dish. Add onion, 4 cloves of the sliced garlic, and 3 tablespoons of water. Cover tightly and cook for 5 minutes or until onion is soft. Then add tomatoes, crushed red pepper, and a pinch of sugar; salt and pepper to taste. Cook an additional 5 minutes. Stuff the eggplant with cheese and the remaining 4 cloves of the sliced garlic. Nestle the eggplant back into the sauce in the casserole dish. Sprinkle fresh mint, basil and parsley over the eggplants and cover. Cook on low heat, turning every 30 minutes for about 90 minutes. Add water if it begins to stick. Sprinkle with more herbs just before serving.

**Recipe Note:** We love this dish. While tasting the eggplant, we look at each other and exclaim, "Can life get any better than this?!" We serve this to family and friends with warm, crusty bread and a nice bottle of Sicilian wine, like a Regaleali Rosso. -Maggie and Matthew

Maggie Wood & Matthew Kurek
The Golden Earthworm Organic Farm
Jamesport, Long Island, New York

# Ginger sesame eggplant

1 medium eggplant
olive oil
1 garlic clove, finely chopped
1 T. peeled, grated ginger
1 T. sesame seed oil

1/4 tsp. hot sauce
1 T. rice vinegar
1/2 tsp. sugar
1/2 tsp. soy sauce
2 T. chopped cilantro

Coat 1 medium eggplant with olive oil and roast at 400 degrees until soft. Allow to cool, then peel, chunk into 1/2 inch dice and mix with any juices that have accumulated. Combine garlic, ginger and sesame oil. Sauté together until translucent. Toss with eggplant chunks and season with hot sauce, rice vinegar, sugar, soy sauce and chopped cilantro. Serve warm or cold.

**Recipe Note:** Ginger sesame eggplant works equally well as a tortilla chip dip or a sauce for soba noodles.

Kristi Hood
Quail Hill Farm
Amagansett, NY

65106-05

# FARM MOUSSAKA

6-8 eggplants, sliced
4 onions, chopped
4 lbs. ground meat or TVP
  (textured vegetable protein)
  and mixed vegetables

2 large cans tomatoes
2 cans tomato paste
spices (garlic, oregano, parsley,
  cinnamon, salt and pepper),
  to taste

Béchamel

12 T. butter ($^3/_4$ cup)
8-10 T. flour (1-$^1/_2$ cups)

4 c. milk
salt and pepper, to taste

Topping

2 c. grated cheese

Sauté eggplant in olive oil; set aside. Sauté onions; set aside. Brown ground meat. Or, sauté mixed vegetables and add soaked TVP. Add onions, tomatoes, tomato paste, spices (Be generous! It's the cinnamon that especially adds the special flavor people will rave about.) Simmer. Layer sautéed eggplant in lightly greased large pan. Make béchamel sauce: melt butter, slowly add flour until you have a uniform paste, stir in milk over low heat, add salt and pepper. Add meat mixture on top of eggplant. Pour béchamel sauce over meat. Sprinkle cheese on top. Bake at 325 degrees for 1 hour.

Catrien van Assendelft
World Hunger Relief Farm
Elm Mott, Texas

# EGGPLANT CAVIAR
## (Freezes beautifully! Defrost for a party!)

1 small eggplant, cubed
1/3 c. chopped green pepper
1 medium onion, chopped
1/4 lb. mushrooms, sliced
  (optional)
2 garlic cloves, crushed
1/3 c. olive oil
1 tsp. salt
1/2 tsp. pepper

1/2 tsp. oregano
1-1/2 tsp. sugar
3 T. pignolis (pine nuts)
6 oz. tomato paste
1/4 c. water
2 T. wine vinegar
1/2 c. green and/or black olives
1/4 c. capers (drained and
  washed)

Combine eggplant, pepper, onion, mushrooms, garlic, and olive oil in a 12 inch skillet. Cover and simmer for 15 minutes. Then add and stir all remaining ingredients into the mixture. Serve hot or cold with crackers or top mixture on pizza dough and bake.

*Freezes beautifully*

*Simmer 25 min.*

Carole Gauger
Maple View Farm
Harwinton, Connecticut

# INDIAN-STYLE EGGPLANT

1 eggplant
3 T. vegetable oil
1 green chili, finely diced
1 onion, diced
1/2 c. green peas

1 tomato, diced
1/2 tsp. chili powder
1/2 tsp. garam masala
1/4 tsp. turmeric
salt to taste

Cut eggplant in half. Cook in microwave until soft. Cut skin off of eggplant. Dice eggplant. Set aside. Heat oil in a pan. Add green chili and onion. Cook until golden brown. Add all other ingredients. Cook until tender. Serve immediately.

**Recipe Note:** Garam Masala, a special South Asian spice blend, is generally added in a small quantity at the end of cooking to add a subtle flavor to the dish.

Jeanine Jenks Farley
Waltham Fields Community Farm
Waltham, Massachusetts

65106-05

# SQUASH OF ALL KINDS

# SQUASH OF ALL KINDS

## SUMMER SQUASH WRAPS

1 head of leaf lettuce (romaine, butter head, or red Grand Rapids)
3-5 small zucchini, yellow squash, or patty pan

3 T. balsamic vinegar, divided
2 T. olive oil
sea salt, to taste
1/2 c. fresh croutons
1/4 c. pine nuts, toasted

Wash lettuce in cold water and discard damaged leaves. Separate leaves (keeping them whole) and store in a plastic bag in the refrigerator. Wash and trim ends of summer squash. Do not peel them. Slice them lengthwise about 1 inch thick. Brush with balsamic vinegar and olive oil (about half of each) and salt. Cook them on a preheated smoky grill over medium heat. Cook several minutes on each side until slightly brown. Remove squash from grill and cube (in about 1 inch cubes). Gently mix with croutons, pine nuts, remaining olive oil and balsamic vinegar. Salt to taste. Place in serving bowl. Place fresh cold lettuce leaves on a serving plate. Let each guest scoop the hot squash mixture and place it in the leaf, rolling it to be eaten like a taco or small burrito.

Penny and Brian Toth
Maple Creek Farm
Yale, Michigan

# EASY, CHEESY SUMMER SQUASH

3 T. vegetable oil or olive oil
1 garlic clove, chopped
1 jalapeño pepper, seeded and
  minced
6 small squash, cut into 1 inch
  chunks

2 tomatoes, chopped (about 3
  cups)
1 c. fresh, frozen, or canned
  corn
salt and pepper, to taste
½ lb. sharp cheddar cheese

In a wide skillet, heat oil over medium heat. Add garlic and jalapeño pepper. Cook 3 minutes or until garlic is fragrant, then add squash. Increase heat to high and cook uncovered for 10 minutes, stirring occasionally. Reduce heat to medium and stir in chopped tomatoes and corn. Cook 10 minutes more, uncovered stirring occasionally. Season with salt and pepper. Remove from heat and sprinkle with cheese. Cover and let cheese melt.

Les Snyder & Monica Helsley
Sunshine Farm
Lagrange, Kentucky

*"Tell me what you eat and I will tell you what you are."*
*Anthelme Brillat-Savarin*

65106-05

# STUFFED ZUCCHINI
## (Hot Italian sausage adds a nice zing!)

4 medium-sized zucchini
squash, cut lengthwise and
cored

2 T. Parmesan cheese

### Stuffing

¼ lb. hot Italian sausage,
cooked, crumbled, and drained
4 oz. goat cheese
4 oz. mozzarella cheese, grated
2 c. diced tomatoes, canned or
fresh

1 tsp. finely chopped fresh basil
1 tsp. salt
1 tsp. pepper

Place the zucchini in a baking dish. Mix stuffing ingredients together. Stuff the halved zucchini with the stuffing mixture, equally distributing it among the 8 halves. Top with Parmesan cheese and bake uncovered at 350 degrees for 30 minutes or until zucchini is thoroughly cooked. Serves 4.

Kelly Saxer
Desert Roots Farm CSA
Queen Creek, Arizona


# FRESH GREEN SOUP
## (Simple, refreshing and healthy!)

2 avocados, peeled and sliced
3 c. apple juice
½ lemon, juiced
2 small zucchini, grated
sprouts, any type
1 celery stalk, diced

¼ c. chopped parsley
2 tsp. tamari
ground ginger, to taste
⅓ c. almonds
⅓ c. sliced mushrooms
(optional)

Mix all ingredients and serve as a cold soup or serve at room temperature.

Deborah Hildebrandt
Be Wise Ranch CSA
San Diego, California

# SAVORY ZUCCHINI BREAD

3 c. grated zucchini with skin
1 medium onion, chopped
1 c. all-purpose baking mix
3 large eggs
½ c. canola oil
½ c. grated cheese

1 small handful fresh basil
  leaves, chopped
1 small handful fresh parsley
  leaves, chopped
1 dash marjoram
1 dash fresh black pepper

Mix all above ingredients and place in an 8 x 8 square greased baking pan and bake at 350 degrees for 30 to 45 minutes, or until top is golden brown. Do not overcook!

Mary Cannavo
Sophia Garden
Amityville, New York

# ZUCCHINI PATTIES

## (An alternative to the traditional beef burger.)

2 c. grated zucchini (squeeze
  to press out excess liquid)
1 egg, beaten
2 T. diced onion

4 T. bread crumbs
1 pinch salt
canola oil

Mix all ingredients in a bowl except oil and divide mixture into 4 patties. Fry in an oiled skillet until brown on both sides and heated through.

**Recipe Note:** Patties can be topped with a slice of cheese

Franz Rulofson, College of the Redwoods
Sustainable Agriculture Farm
Shively, California

65106-05

# APPLE, ZUCCHINI, PEPPER SALAD

½ c. Italian dressing
1 tsp. dried basil
ground pepper
3 medium apples, cored and diced
1 medium red onion, peeled and thinly sliced

1 medium green pepper, cut into matchsticks
1 lb. zucchini, cut into matchsticks

In a large salad bowl, combine dressing, basil and ground pepper. Add apples and vegetables and toss lightly to coat. Cover and chill at least 4 hours. Just before serving, toss again and serve cold. Serves 8.

Paula Langenstein
Maple Creek Farm
Yale, Michigan


# ZUCCHINI SOUP

1 lb. sweet sausage (casing removed)
2 c. celery, cut into small pieces
2 lbs. zucchini sliced (can mix in other squash also)
1 c. chopped onion

2 (16-oz.) cans tomatoes
2 tsp. salt
1 tsp. oregano
1 tsp. sugar
¼ tsp. garlic powder
½ tsp. basil
2 green peppers, chopped

Brown the sausage in a large pot, drain off fat, add celery and cook 10 minutes. Add all other ingredients except peppers. Simmer and cook 20 to 30 minutes. Add green peppers and cook covered simmering for 10 minutes.

Carole Gauger
Maple View Farm
Harwinton, Connecticut

# EASY STUFFED ZUCCHINI

½ lb. ground beef, pork or
  turkey (or mix)
½ onion
fresh garlic
1 large tomato
1 T. cooking sherry or red wine
½ c. cooked rice

fresh herbs
salt and pepper, to taste
1 large zucchini, cut length-wise
  and cored
½ c. grated or shredded
  cheese

Sauté ground meat, onion, and garlic, draining fat. Add chopped tomato continue to sauté, then add wine or sherry. Let mixture simmer about 3 minutes. Add rice, season to taste with herbs. Put mixture into zucchini, place in a 9 x 13 baking pan, and sprinkle with favorite cheese. Bake at 350 degrees uncovered for about 40 to 60 minutes until squash is tender.

Lilly Cosker
Pitcher Mountain CSA
Stoddard, New Hampshire

65106-05

# MIM'S VEGETABLE MELANGE
## (Featuring yellow squash and zucchini!)

3-4 T. olive oil
2-5 garlic cloves
1 onion, chopped
1 large, 2 med. or 4 small
  zucchini or yellow squash or
  both
1-1/2 T. fresh basil
1-1/2 tsp. dried oregano
1/2 tsp. sweet Hungarian
  paprika

chunky sea salt
black pepper
3 c. mushrooms, stems
  removed, caps thinly sliced
(10-oz.) fresh or frozen
  greens - spinach, kale,
  collards
sun-dried tomatoes
rice or pasta, fully cooked

Sauté squash, onions and minced garlic in 1/2 the oil for about 10 minutes. Toss in herbs, salt and pepper and sprinkle with 1 to 2 tablespoons of water. Cover pan and cook over high heat for about 2 minutes. Then reduce heat and cook covered until the veggies are soft but not mushy. Meanwhile, sauté mushrooms in remaining oil until tender and a little brown on the edges. Defrost greens if frozen and squeeze out the water. Add mushrooms and greens to squash mixture. Stir and cook together for about 15 more minutes to blend flavors.

**Recipe Note:** I added some cut up sun-dried tomatoes for color and served this over rice or pasta. -Mim

Mim Golub Scalin
Sprout CSA/Phillips Organic Farm
Richmond, Virginia

# RISOTTO IN ROASTED ACORN SQUASH
## (With fennel and shiitake mushrooms)

2 large acorn squash, halved
and seeded
3 T. butter
1 c. minced onion
1-1/2 c. minced fennel bulb or
celery stalks
1 large garlic clove, minced
1-1/2 c. farro, cracked spelt or
cracked wheat (or 1-1/4 cup
Arborio rice)

1/3 c. sherry or white wine
4-1/2 c. water or vegetable
broth (or 3-3/4 cups if using
Arborio rice)
1 tsp. salt
1/4 c. grated Parmesan cheese
salt and black pepper
2 c. chopped shiitake
mushrooms

Slice a bit off of the outside of each squash half, so they won't wobble on the plates. Bake, flesh side down, at 400 degrees on a baking sheet for 1 hour or until flesh is tender. Melt 1-1/2 tablespoons of butter in a large skillet over medium heat. Add the onion and fennel or celery and cook, stirring occasionally, for about 8 minutes, or until they have softened. Add the garlic and sauté 2 minutes more. Add the farro, cracked spelt, cracked wheat, or Arborio rice and sauté, stirring for 1 minute. Add the sherry or wine and continue stirring. When the wine has absorbed, add 1/2 cup of water or broth, and one teaspoon of salt. Stir as the mixture simmers. Add another 1/2 cup of water or broth, once the first is absorbed, and stir occasionally. Continue adding liquid 1/2 cup at a time, until it is absorbed, about 30 minutes, or about 20 minutes if using Arborio rice. Add the Parmesan and salt and pepper, to taste. In a small skillet, melt the remaining 1-1/2 tablespoon of butter. Sauté the mushrooms with the butter over medium heat, stirring often, for 5 minutes. Add salt and pepper to taste. Fold half of the mushrooms into the farro and reserve the rest. Place the squash halves cut side up on 4 dinner plates and fill with risotto. Top with the reserved mushrooms and serve immediately. Serves 4.

**Recipe Note:** We hosted a dinner for Jared's parents and friends in Jared's little apartment in Boston right after our engagement. Jared refers to it as "his most successful meal ever." This was the featured dish! -Annaliese

Annaliese Franz and Jared Shaw
Waltham Fields Community Farm
Waltham, Massachusetts

65106-05

# BUTTERNUT SQUASH SOUP
## (With red bell pepper purée!)

| | |
|---|---|
| 1 T. oil | 1 bay leaf |
| 4 c. butternut squash, peeled, | 1 tsp. oregano |
| and cut into 1 inch pieces | 1/4 tsp. nutmeg |
| 1 lb. onions, chopped | 1/2 tsp. salt |
| 4 c. chicken or vegetable broth | 1/4 tsp. pepper |
| 2 T. maple syrup | |

Sauté oil, squash and onions. Add broth, maple syrup and spices and cook until squash is soft. Remove the bay leaf and purée soup in food processor or blender. Thin if necessary with water or stock. Serve with red bell pepper purée 8 to 10 servings.

### Red Bell Pepper Purée

| | |
|---|---|
| 1 roasted red bell pepper | 1/2 tsp. ground coriander |
| 3 T. broth | |

Purée above ingredients.

**Recipe Note:** This soup is served each year at the Davis Art Center holiday sale in December with rave reviews! -Patricia

Patricia Carpenter
Eatwell Farm
Dixon, California

# BUTTERNUT SQUASH AND WHITE BEAN SOUP
## (Kid-approved!)

2 lbs. white beans
4 c. chopped celery
8 c. chopped onion
12 garlic cloves, chopped
1 large piece of fresh ginger, shredded

2-4 T. canola oil
1 gal. stock, vegetable or chicken
8 c. butternut squash, peeled and cubed
salt and pepper, to taste

Sort the beans (looking for stones and dirt) and wash them. Soak the beans overnight or put them in a pot with enough water to cover the beans with 2 inches of water, bring to a boil and allow to sit for 1 hour with a cover. Sauté the celery, onion, garlic and ginger in the canola oil. Add the stock and beans. Bring the mixture to a boil and reduce to a simmer. Peel, remove the seeds and cube butternut squash. Place squash in the pot. Add salt and pepper to taste. Simmer 2 hours, stirring every ½ hour or so, until squash is not longer in cubes and beans are done.

**Recipe Note:** If the squash is cooked separately, it can be puréed before combining with the beans for a smoother soup. Otherwise, the squash chunks cook down as the soup simmers.

Margaret Pennings
Common Harvest Farms
Osceola, Wisconsin

65106-05

# BUTTERNUT SQUASH CASSEROLE
## (A simple yet special autumn side dish!)

1 butternut squash
2 garlic cloves
1 onion, chopped (or leeks,
  cleaned well and chopped)
1 T. olive oil

½ c. whole-wheat bread crumbs
¼ tsp. each of ground pepper
  and salt
3 T. grated Parmesan cheese

Cut squash in half lengthwise and remove seeds. On a rimmed cookie sheet, lined with aluminum foil, place squash with the rind facing up. Bake at 350 degrees for 45 to 60 minutes or until very soft. Let cool for 5 minutes and scoop out the insides, being careful not to scoop the outer skin. Place the squash in a casserole dish. Sauté garlic and onion in the olive oil, and mix into the squash. Stir in bread crumbs, pepper and salt. Sprinkle cheese on top and cover the dish with foil or a lid. Bake at 350 degrees for 10 minutes (or longer if ingredients have cooled). Serves 6 as a side dish.

**Recipe Note:** Instead of using whole-wheat bread crumbs, I cut up one piece of whole-wheat toast. It works great! -Mari

Mari Mielcarski
Eatwell Farm
Dixon, California

# BAKED BUTTERNUT SQUASH AND APPLES

1 butternut squash
3-4 apples
1/2 c. butter

2 T. flour
1/2 c. brown sugar
1/2 tsp. cinnamon

Peel squash and cut in half lengthwise. Remove and discard seeds. Slice each half crosswise into 3/8 inch thick slices. Peel and core apples. Cut in half lengthwise. Slice each half crosswise into 3/8 inch thick slices. Arrange the slices in two rows in a 9 x 13 inch baking dish, alternating squash and apple slices in each row. Melt the butter and mix in the flour, brown sugar and cinnamon. Pour over squash and apples. Cover baking dish and bake at 350 degrees for 1 hour, or until tender.

friends of Old Maids Farm
Glastonbury, Connecticut


# THE SIMPLEST BUTTERNUT SQUASH

1 medium butternut squash,
   halved and seeded.

1 T. butter
2 T. brown sugar

Turn halved squash upside down onto a cookie sheet. Bake at 350 degrees until it begins to soften, about 30 to 45 minutes. Remove squash from the oven and keep it upside down so flesh is facing upwards. Place butter and brown sugar into the squash and return to the oven for about 20 minutes more.

Trish Hewitt
H & H Organic Farms
Raleigh, North Carolina

65106-05

# BUTTERNUT SQUASH PIZZA

1 medium butternut squash
handful of fresh sage leaves
2 sprigs of thyme
salt and pepper
1 medium onion
3 slices of bacon

1 c. shredded mozzarella cheese
1 c. shredded Gruyere cheese
1 lemon
olive oil
1-2 T. butter
1 lb. pizza dough

Cut the squash in half, lengthwise, scoop out the seeds and season with salt and pepper. Drizzle with olive oil and place face down in a baking dish. Cook until easily pierced with a fork, roughly 45 minutes. Cool, then scoop out flesh. Mash the squash with a bit of butter if it needs to be creamier. Chop the thyme and a few of the sage leaves and mix into the squash, season with more salt and pepper to taste. Caramelize the onion and cook the bacon. Grate both of the cheeses and mix them together before adding to the pizza. To bake the pizza, precook the dough on a pizza stone or greased cookie sheet so that it has a bit of golden brown color to it, at 400 degrees for about 7 to 10 minutes. Remove the pizza from the oven and add the toppings: spread the squash on the dough, as you would tomato sauce, only thicker, add the cheeses and top with the onion and bacon. Return to the oven and when the pizza seems nearly done (about 15 minutes), sauté the rest of the sage leaves in a bit of butter for a minute or two. Sage leaves burn easily, if they begin to color and look cooked, they are done. Remove the pizza from the oven, scatter the cooked sage leaves and squeeze a bit of lemon juice on top and serve.

**Recipe Note:** This is more of a flat bread than a pizza and is decidedly richer than your "run of the mill" pizza.

Tessa van der Werff
Fairview Gardens
Goleta, California

# DELICATA SQUASH WITH WILD RICE
## (The creamy walnut sauce makes this delicious!)

2 delicata squash
1 T. plus ½ tsp. salt
½ tsp. black pepper
1 T. olive oil
1 small red onion, diced
½ c. dry sherry
2 c. cooked wild rice

½ bunch parsley, chopped
½ c. sour cream
½ c. walnuts, toasted
⅓ c. cream cheese
½ c. milk
1 T. lemon juice
1 T. cinnamon

Halve the squash and scrape out the seeds. Lightly salt and pepper the squash. Arrange squash, cut side down, in a baking dish with about 1 inch of water. Cover and microwave until a fork can easily pierce the flesh about 15 minutes. Meanwhile, heat oil in a large skillet over medium heat. Add the onion and sauté until soft, about 10 minutes. Stir in the sherry and pepper and simmer 3 minutes. Stir in the cooked wild rice and heat through. Add the parsley and mix well. Keep warm. In a blender, purée the sour cream, toasted walnuts, cream cheese, milk, lemon juice, cinnamon and ½ teaspoon salt. Add a little extra milk if needed to make a smooth sauce. Reserve. Spoon the wild rice mixture into the squash cavities, pour walnut sauce over squash and serve immediately.

**Recipe Note:** The sauce for this dish has a very interesting mix of fall flavors from the combination of cinnamon, lemon juice and sour cream.

Solyssa Visalli
Cop Copi Farms
La Grand, Oregon

*"It's difficult to think of anything but pleasant thoughts while eating a homegrown tomato."*

*Lewis Grizzard*

65106-05

# CREAMY PUMPKIN SOUP
## (Great for an autumn picnic!)

### Pumpkin Purée

2 c. fresh pumpkin, cooked and
  skinned

To make pumpkin purée from a whole pumpkin: Cut the pumpkin in half and remove seeds and strings. Place skin side up on a lightly oiled baking sheet. Bake at 400 degrees until the skin is wrinkled and the flesh is soft. The time depends on the size of the pumpkin but an average-sized pumpkin takes about an hour. Remove from oven and cool. The skin should peel off easily and the pumpkin flesh can be cut into cubes or puréed.

### Soup

3 T. butter
1/2 c. chopped onions
1 tsp. salt
1 T. sugar
1/4 tsp. nutmeg

1/4 tsp. ground pepper
3 c. chicken broth
1/2 c. half and half or fat-free
  half and half

Melt butter over medium heat in large soup pot. Add onions and cook until clear but not brown. Add the pumpkin and remaining ingredients except half and half. Cook for about 5 minutes. Ladle the soup into a blender and purée until smooth. The soup can be made ahead of time and kept in the refrigerator for a couple of days. Just before serving, add the half and half and stir. You may add chives or other garnishes as you wish.

Nancy Kalman
Picklings & Pumpkins LLC
Spring Hills, KS

# ANNE'S PUMPKIN SOUP

1 pumpkin, about 3 pounds
1 c. chopped onions
1/2 c. chopped celery

4 T. melted ghee
4 c. chicken broth
salt and pepper

Slice pumpkin in half vertically and remove all seeds and strings. Place pumpkin in a baking dish. Add about 1/2 inch of water. Bake at 350 degrees for 1 hour or until tender. Cut into strips and remove shell. Place peeled pumpkin in a bowl. In a large saucepan, sauté onion and celery in ghee until translucent. Meanwhile, purée pumpkin in a food processor until smooth, adding broth as needed to easily purée. Purée sautéed vegetables if a smooth soup is desired. Return to saucepan and add remaining broth and vegetables. Simmer and season to taste. Makes 8 servings.

**Recipe Note:** Ghee is a clarified butter without any solid milk particles or water.

Anne Morgan
Lakes of the Valley CSA/Midheaven Farms
Park Rapids, Minnesota

65106-05

# STUFFED SPAGHETTI SQUASH

1 spaghetti squash, sliced
   lengthwise, seeds scraped
   out
1 c. chopped onion
1 clove garlic, grated
2 T. olive oil
1 zucchini (approx. 1 inch
   diameter.), grated into
   strands (about 1 cup)

2-3 tomatoes, chopped, shake
   liquid out
herbs: basil, parsley, marjoram,
   oregano - one or more
optional cheeses: Parmesan,
   Romano, etc.
oil

Bake squash at 375 degrees cut side down in 1 inch of water. May also bake on an oiled tray for about 40 minutes or until you can pierce with fork, or may boil until fairly tender. Meanwhile, sauté onions and garlic in olive oil until soft. Add grated zucchini and stir for a minute. Stir in chopped tomatoes and herbs. Cook a few minutes trying to absorb juices (or drain). Salt and pepper to taste. When squash is soft, carefully scoop loose the innards, trying to retain strands. Lumps should squish nicely between fingers! Carefully mix squash strands into veggie mixture, then fold approximately half of this mixture into each squash half shell. Stir in some grated cheese as well or just top with Parmesan, light or heavy coating. Bake for another 15 to 20 minutes in shells to heat and serve.

**Recipe Note:** The seeds are great, too with a light oil coating, baked about 20 minutes.

Jill Fish
Pitcher Mountain CSA
Stoddard, New Hampshire

# EASY SPAGHETTI SQUASH
## (This will make a vegetarian out of meat-lovers!)

1 large, hard, pale yellow
  spaghetti squash
butter or olive oil

garlic powder
salt and fresh ground black
  pepper, to taste

Cut squash in half, scoop out just the seeds in the center with a large spoon, place it flesh side up on a cookie sheet. Liberally spread with butter or olive oil, sprinkle with garlic powder, salt, and fresh ground black pepper. Let it bake at 400 degrees for 25 minutes (more or less depending on the size of your squash). When you take it out of the oven, scoop out the wonderful, soft, nutty flesh. It can be used as a side dish or as the meal with French bread garlic toast!

**Recipe Note:** Add Italian seasoning and Parmesan cheese, when serving it with Italian foods. Other combinations: add curry powder and cumin or fresh garlic and fresh basil.

Amy Stroud
BAKA Farm
Campbell, Texas

65106-05

# SQUASH POLENTA

Puréed Squash

3 lbs. winter squash, halved
  and seeded
3 T. olive oil

6 garlic cloves, unpeeled
6-8 fresh sage leaves, chopped

Halve the squash and scoop out the seeds. Roast it face up on a cookie sheet or roasting pan with the garlic cloves in the cavity and drizzled with the olive oil and sprinkle with chopped sage. (Acorn, delicata or festival are ideal squash for this recipe.) Roast at 375 degrees for 1 to 2 hours depending on the size of your squash. The flesh should be very soft. Remove from the oven and cool just until you can handle them enough to scoop out the flesh. Transfer scooped squash and garlic cloves (peel removed) to a processor and purée.

Polenta

2-$^3$/$_4$ c. chicken or vegetable
  stock
1-$^1$/$_2$ c. water
1-2 T. salt
1-$^1$/$_2$ c. polenta (coarse
  cornmeal)

2 fresh sage leaves, minced
$^3$/$_4$ c. freshly grated Parmesan
  cheese
salt and pepper, to taste

To make the polenta, combine the stock, water and salt in a large, heavy bottomed pot and bring to a boil. Slowly whisk in the cornmeal, reducing the heat so it just continues to simmer. Stir it often. It takes about 20 minutes before it begins to thicken. Stir in more chopped sage and 3 cups of the squash purée. Stir in cheese and adjust seasonings. Serves 6 to 8.

Linda Halley
Harmony Valley Farm
Viroqua, Wisconsin

# MAPLE SQUASH

1 winter squash              1 T. butter
2 T. pure Vermont maple syrup    salt and pepper, to taste

Wash squash and cut in half. Clean out seeds and pulp. Steam until soft and the skin easily peels off. Run under cold water until cool enough to handle. Add 2 tablespoons pure Vermont maple syrup and 1 tablespoon butter for each medium squash as well as salt and pepper to taste. Mash or purée and enjoy! (Alternately, when squash is in half and cleaned, add 2 tablespoons of pure Vermont maple syrup and 1 tablespoon butter to each half. Bake at 375 degrees for 45 minutes or until soft.) Enjoy! Serves 2 to 3.

Sara Schlosser
Sandiwood Farm
Wolcott, Vermont

# WINTER SQUASH CHOWDER
## (Cheese and cream make this chowder rich!)

2 T. vegetable oil
1-1/2 c. chopped onion
7-8 c. butternut squash or
   pumpkin, peeled, seeded and
   cubed
1/4-1/2 lb. chopped ham or
   turkey ham
4 c. water or chicken broth
2 bay leaves

1 c. diced carrots
1 c. diced celery
1 c. shelled edamame or diced
   green beans
1 c. shredded sharp cheddar
   cheese
1-2 c. rich milk or cream
salt and pepper, to taste

Sauté onion in oil. Add squash, diced ham, broth, and bay leaves. Simmer until squash is tender about 20 minutes. Use potato masher to break up squash chunks. In a separate pot, cook carrots, celery and beans in 2 cups of water until just tender. Add the vegetables, cheese, and milk to the squash and heat gently while stirring. Season with salt and pepper to taste.

**Recipe Note:** Other fresh herbs such as sage or thyme can be added.

Trish Mumme
Garden Patch Produce CSA
Alexandria, Ohio

# TOMATOES

# TOMATOES

## PEELING AND SEEDING TOMATOES

Peeling and seeding tomatoes for fresh tomato sauce is a slightly tedious procedure, but one that ought to be mastered nonetheless. To peel and seed fresh tomatoes, bring a large pot of water to boil over high heat. Using a paring knife, cut a shallow cross into the bottom of each tomato. Submerge the tomatoes in the boiling water for 15 to 20 seconds, depending on ripeness (the riper the tomatoes, the less time they need in the water). Immediately remove the tomatoes and transfer to a colander. Rinse with cold water until cool. Using a paring knife, remove the stem and core and discard. Slip the skin from the tomato and discard. Cutting across the tomato rather than from top to bottom, slice the tomato in half. With a fine wire mesh or strainer set over a bowl, gently squeeze the seeds (and juice) from the tomato so that the strainer catches the seeds and the juice runs into the bowl. Do this with all the tomatoes. Discard the seeds and use the tomato juice in the recipe. The tomatoes can then be cut into the desired shape and size according to the recipe directions.

Note that 3 pounds of tomatoes are approximately equal to 7 large tomatoes.

Karen Vollmecke
Vollmecke Orchards CSA
West Brandywine, Pennsylvania

*"When in doubt, use thyme."*

*Grass Roots Herb Society*

# Salsa cruda de tomatillos

1 lb. fresh tomatillos, husked
1 small-medium onion, chopped
2 garlic cloves, roughly chopped
2 jalapeño peppers, tops
   removed (not seeded)

½ c. loosely packed cilantro
   (fresh)
pinch of salt

Process all ingredients in blender or food processor using pulse button, until puréed but still somewhat chunky. Serve at once. Keeps for about 2 weeks in refrigerator in a tightly closed glass jar.

Catherine J. Harley
Four Springs Farm
Royalton, Vermont


# Tomatillo and corn soup

3 T. unsalted butter
1 medium onion, finely chopped
5 tomatillos, husked and
   quartered
1 T. minced garlic
6 ears corn, roasted and
   removed from the cob
4 c. chicken broth or vegetable
   stock
6 fresh cilantro sprigs plus
   additional cilantro for
   garnish

¼ c. diced green chilies or
   other hot peppers
¼ c. packed chopped spinach
   (or other greens)
1 T. sugar
tortilla chips, garnish
sour cream, garnish

Melt butter in large heavy pot over medium heat. Add onion, tomatillos and garlic. Sauté 5 minutes. Mix in most of the corn, 3 cups of stock, and cilantro sprigs. Purée mixture in blender in batches. Return purée to pot and bring to simmer. Add peppers, spinach, sugar, remaining corn and remaining cup of stock to soup. Simmer 15 minutes. Season to taste with salt. Ladle soup into bowls; sprinkle with tortilla chips. Top with sour cream and chopped cilantro. Serve.

Walt Forrester, Parker House Inn
Four Springs Farm
Royalton, Vermont

65106-05

# TOMATILLO CHICKEN

6 free-range skinless, boneless chicken breast halves
4 c. chicken broth
1 medium onion, chopped
2-3 canned or dried hot peppers
1 bay leaf

2-3 garlic cloves, crushed
1 lb. whole tomatillos, husked
1/3 c. chopped fresh cilantro
1 tsp. sugar (optional)
salt to taste
sour cream, garnish

In a covered large Dutch oven simmer chicken in broth with onion, peppers, garlic, and bay leaf for 15 minutes after reaching a boil. Remove from heat and let cool 15 minutes. Remove chicken from pot and set aside until cool enough to handle. Meanwhile, add tomatillos to the pot, bring to a boil over medium-high heat, and boil the tomatillos, uncovered for 10 minutes or until soft. With a slotted spoon, transfer the tomatillos and peppers to a blender, add the cilantro and purée. Pour the mixture back into the stock and mix well. Season to taste. Pull chicken breasts apart into large chunks, add back to the tomatillo mixture, and simmer until sauce thickens slightly, about 10 minutes. Serve hot with tortilla chips, guacamole or avocado slices. Garnish with a dollop of sour cream.

Catherine J. Harley
Four Springs Farm
Royalton, Vermont

# SALSA VERDE

5-½ c. chopped tomatillos
1 c. chopped onions
1 c. chopped green chilis
4 garlic cloves
2 T. cilantro

2 tsp. cumin
½ tsp. salt
½ tsp. red pepper
1 c. vinegar
¼ c. lime juice

Mix ingredients until blended.

**Recipe Note:** This is beautiful with purple tomatillos, giving a great blend of sweet and spicy! This recipe was given out to our CSA customers last year and became a favorite. -Pennie

Pennie Halpin
Halpin Highlands Family Farm
Kaleva, Michigan

65106-05

# Italian Bread Salad
## (An easy evening meal on a hot day!)

### Salad

2 c. sliced fresh vine-ripe
  tomatoes
2 c. garlic croutons
1 c. sliced fresh whole-milk
  mozzarella cheese

1/4 c. sliced fresh basil leaves
balsamic vinegar
olive oil
fresh minced garlic
fresh ground pepper

Toss tomatoes, croutons, cheese and basil leaves in a bowl. Sprinkle with vinegar, oil, garlic, and pepper. For a more elegant presentation, leave basil leaves whole and arrange tomatoes and cheese individually over croutons on salad plate. Sprinkle with garlic and drizzle with oil and vinegar. Serves 2 as a light summer dinner or more as a side dish.

### Garlic Croutons

Make your own croutons by slicing sourdough bread, brush with melted garlic butter, cut into cubes, and toast on a cookie sheet at 375 degrees, turning occasionally, until brown.

**Recipe Note:** It is absolutely forbidden to serve bread salad with tomatoes that are not truly vine ripe!

Jeane Duffer
Barklee Farm
Sagle, Idaho

# TOMATO SALAD
## (Great on a hot summer day!)

2 large tomatoes, sliced
½ onion, sliced thinly
1 T. olive oil
1 T. apple cider vinegar or red
    wine vinegar

1 tsp. salt
1 garlic clove, crushed

In a salad bowl, add tomatoes and onions. In a separate bowl, combine olive oil, vinegar, salt and garlic to make a vinaigrette. Pour the vinaigrette over the tomatoes and onions. Toss. Add additional salt to taste. Refrigerate 10 to 15 minutes before serving. Serves 4.

Kelly Saxer
Desert Roots Farm CSA
Queen Creek, Arizona

# GARDEN FRESH TOMATO SOUP
## (A food processor makes this recipe quick and easy!)

1 T. olive oil
2 garlic cloves, minced
2 carrots, chopped
1 medium onion, chopped
2 celery stalks, chopped
2 qts. tomatoes, chopped
¼ c. fresh basil
1 T. finely chopped fresh
    oregano

1 T. sugar
sea salt and fresh ground
    pepper, to taste
1 tsp. tamari or soy sauce, to
    taste
Parmesan or Romano cheese,
    grated

Heat oil in skillet. Sauté garlic, carrots, onion and celery. Add tomatoes and simmer 20 minutes. Add basil, oregano, sugar, salt, pepper, and soy sauce. Simmer 5 to 10 minutes longer. Serve with cheese. Serves 8.

**Recipe Note:** Cut down on your chopping time! Use your food processor to chop carrots, onions, celery, garlic and fresh herbs.

Jackie Good
RC Organic Farm CSA
Lenox, Michigan

65106-05

# MAGGIE'S FRESH TOMATO SAUCE
## (Great on a hot day; no stove needed!)

3 lbs. tomatoes, peeled and
  diced
3 cloves garlic, minced
1/2 c. olive oil
1/4 c. chopped fresh basil

2 T. minced fresh parsley
1/2 tsp. red pepper flakes
2 T. balsamic vinegar
1 tsp. coarse salt
penne pasta

Combine all ingredients except salt and pasta. Let it sit in a large non-aluminum bowl at room temperature, covered, for 30 minutes, up to 6 hours. Prepare pasta. Toss with sauce and add salt just before serving.

**Recipe Note:** I love to prepare this first thing in the morning and let it sit on the counter all day. It fills the kitchen with the most heavenly aroma and keeps me away from the stove! I usually toss with pasta, but I can just as easily drain the tomatoes and make bruschetta with this versatile sauce. -Maggie

Maggie Wood
The Golden Earthworm Organic Farm
Jamesport, Long Island, New York

# HEIRLOOM TOMATO SOUP

## (Black beans add a nice twist to this classic soup!)

15-20 juicy tomatoes
1 bulb of garlic, peeled and minced
3-4 onions (Walla Walla or storage types)
2-3 sweet peppers
3-4 carrots
4-5 celery stems or 1 celeriac root

2-3 c. cooked or canned black beans
olive oil
1 handful of basil, cut into small pieces
1 handful of oregano, cut into small pieces
salt and pepper to taste

Cut all vegetables into small soup-sized pieces including the tomatoes. Sauté onions and garlic in olive oil, then add carrots, peppers and celery. Add chopped tomatoes when the other vegetables are soft. Heat until tomato juices are flowing freely. Add herbs, bean, salt and pepper. Simmer for 10 to 15 minutes to allow flavors to mingle. Serve with hearty whole grain bread or crackers.

**Recipe Note:** This soup is a great way to use up split and over ripening tomatoes during peak season. Heirlooms like Brandywine are excellent for this soup when they are in season!

Ryan Voiland
Red Fire Farm
Granby, Massachusetts

65106-05

# TOMATO AND VEGETABLE SALAD

tomatoes, sliced or quartered
  lengthwise
onion, sliced into rings 1/4 inch
  thick
green, red or yellow pepper,
  sliced

cauliflower florets (raw)
broccoli florets (raw)
cucumber slices
celery
garlic

Marinade

apple cider or rice vinegar
1/4-1/2 c. water
1/2 c. oil, or more, depending on
  the amount of vegetables

salt and pepper to taste

Cut or slice vegetables and place them into a bowl. Pour marinade over vegetables. Marinate vegetable combination for at least 4 hours. This salad mix will keep refrigerated for several days.

**Recipe Note:** A delicious recipe from a friend of the farm! -Jinny

Jinny Cleland
Four Springs Farm
Royalton, Vermont


# CHERRY TOMATO PASTA SAUCE

1 lb. any type of cherry
  tomatoes, cut in half
1/2-3/4 c. any combination of
  chopped: onions, garlic,
  celery, mushroom and/or
  pepper of contrasting color

olive oil
1/2 c. chopped basil
1 T. sugar
salt, to taste
freshly grated Parmesan
  cheese

Sauté all the vegetables in a small amount of olive oil until they are just tender. Add a generous amount of chopped basil, sugar and salt. Serve over pasta with freshly grated Parmesan cheese.

Friends of Four Springs Farm
Royalton, Vermont

# MARINATED TOMATO SALAD
## (Enjoy with a crusty loaf of bread!)

8 tomatoes, sliced
1 onion, chopped
1/4 c. minced fresh parsley
1/4 c. minced fresh Red Rubin
   basil

1/4 c. olive oil
2 T. cider vinegar
1 garlic clove, minced
1 tsp. maple sugar
1 tsp. salt

Chop all ingredients and marinate for 30 minutes.

Rusty & Claire Orner
Quiet Creek Herb Farm
Brookville, Pennsylvania


# THYME-SPIKED TOMATO SOUP

2 garlic cloves, crushed
2 T. olive oil
2 T. flour
4 large tomatoes, skinned and
   chopped
4 sprigs of fresh thyme

1-2 pinches baking soda
   (optional)
1 pinch sucanat
3 c. milk
4 basil leaves
salt and pepper to taste

Sauté garlic in oil. Sprinkle in flour and form paste. Add tomatoes and thyme, simmer for 30 minutes. Remove from heat; add basil and blend into purée. Add baking soda and sucanat. Return to heat and add milk. Serve hot or chilled.

**Recipe Note:** Sucanat (Sugar Cane Natural) is sugar in its most natural form. It is extracted from the sugar cane and the freshly squeezed juice is evaporated by a special Swiss process. Only the water is removed. This process preserves all of the molasses. Sucanat is organically grown with no added preservatives and additives.

Rusty & Claire Orner
Quiet Creek Herb Farm
Brookville, Pennsylvania

65106-05

# FRESH BASIL PASTA SAUCE
## (Don't dry basil; freeze it!)

### Frozen Basil Cubes

2 c. fresh, washed and dried
basil leaves (no stems)
1 T. fresh lemon juice (to
preserve color)

¼ c. vegetable or canola oil

Place the basil leaves and lemon juice in a blender. Add the oil and allow the blender to chop the leaves. Add more oil if necessary to make the blades spin. Blend for 30 to 60 seconds on medium speed. Pour the basil mixture into ice cube trays and freeze overnight. Transfer the cubes to storage bags or containers for use all year long!

### Basil Sauce

salt
1 lb. pasta
2 T. olive oil

2-3 garlic cloves, finely chopped
3 basil cubes (see above)

Boil water and add salt for your choice of pasta (either packaged or fresh homemade). Cook pasta according to the directions. While the pasta is cooking, measure 2 tablespoons of olive oil into a skillet. Add 2 to 3 cloves of finely chopped garlic. Cook until golden. Place 3 basil cubes into the pan for each pound of pasta. Turn off the heat and allow the cubes to melt slowly. Add salt to the basil sauce to taste. Drain the pasta and place the cooked pasta back into the same pot. Add the basil sauce to the pasta and stir well. Add fresh ground pepper to taste.

**Recipe Note:** You may use ¼ cup of Parmesan cheese (more or less to taste) as a salt substitute when tossing the drained pasta with the melted basil sauce.

Julie Vitale
Jupazza Specialty Products/Vitale Farms CSA
Rochester Hills, Michigan

# SAUTÉED CHERRY TOMATOES WITH FETA CHEESE

2 T. extra-virgin olive oil
1 medium onion
1 pt. cherry tomatoes
12 large pitted kalamata olives

1 T. chopped basil or parsley
freshly ground black pepper
2 oz. crumbled feta cheese
  (about ½ cup)

Heat the oil in a large skillet. Add onion and sauté until golden, about 5 minutes. Raise heat to medium high and add tomatoes. Cook just until tomatoes are heated through and skins are beginning to brown in spots, about 2 minutes. Add olives, herbs and pepper to taste. Transfer to a serving bowl. Sprinkle with cheese and serve immediately.

Marlene Washington
Eatwell Farm
Dixon, California


# CITY SLICKER TOMATO SOUP

equal parts of tomatoes and
  milk (8-10 tomatoes makes a
  good batch)
¾ c. diced celery

½ c. diced onions
½-¾ lb. bacon, chopped
⅛ tsp. soda

Scald and skin tomatoes. Dice into soup pot. Simmer. Sauté celery and onions in a small amount of butter or margarine. Fry bacon. Drain grease. Heat an equivalent amount of milk in a separate pan. When tomatoes are tender add the soda. Pour the cooked tomatoes into the warm milk, slowly, stirring continually. Add remaining ingredients. Add seasonings to taste such as: pepper, dill, garlic powder, onion powder or celery flakes.

**Recipe Note:** A city attorney for Sioux Falls, South Dakota gave us this awesome tomato soup recipe. This soup is a delicious and easy way to use extra tomatoes. Put the simmered tomatoes through a colander if your family minds the tomato seeds. -Harriet

Harriet Kattenberg
Seedtime & Harvest
Hull, Iowa

65106-05

# TOMATO BITES
## (A great summer appetizer!)

1 lb. bacon, chopped and fried crisp (can substitute with bacon bits)
1/2 c. miracle whip salad dressing
1/3 c. finely chopped green onions
3 T. Parmesan cheese
2 T. finely chopped parsley
cherry tomatoes

Mix all ingredients except cherry tomatoes. Slice tomatoes in half. Remove pulp with a melon-baller. Fill with stuffing.

**Recipe Note:** Try stuffing cute, little cherry tomatoes with this rich stuffing, and children may change their minds about tomatoes!

Harriet Kattenberg
Seedtime & Harvest
Hull, Iowa

*"Many people have the wrong idea of what constitutes true happiness. It is not attained through self-gratification but through fidelity to a worthy cause."*

Helen Keller

# ROASTED TOMATO AND RED PEPPER GAZPACHO

2-1/2 lbs. tomatoes
2-3 large bell peppers, divided
2 medium red onions, divided
1/4 c. olive oil
1/2 tsp. salt
1/2 c. chopped parsley
1-1/2 c. water, divided

1-1/2 T. sherry vinegar
1/2 tsp. hot pepper sauce
white pepper (optional)
1/2 large cucumber, peeled,
   seeded and finely chopped,
   about 1 cup
olive oil

Core tomatoes and squeeze gently to remove some of the seeds. Place tomatoes upright in a large roasting pan. Cut 2-1/2 peppers and 1-1/2 onions into 1 inch pieces and scatter around (but not on top of) tomatoes. Drizzle 1/4 cup oil over vegetables and sprinkle with salt. Roast vegetables at 450 degrees, uncovered, until soft, about 45 to 60 minutes. In food processor, purée half of vegetables and juices in pan with half of parsley until smooth. Add 1/2 cup water and process until very smooth. Repeat with remaining vegetables, parsley and 1/2 cup water. Cover and chill at least 6 hours or overnight. Mix together remaining 1/2 cup water, vinegar and hot pepper sauce and stir into gazpacho. Season to taste with salt and white pepper, if desired. Finely chop remaining bell pepper and onion and combine with cucumber. Top each serving with diced vegetables and drizzle with olive oil. Serves 4.

**Recipe Note:** Red peppers visually complement this tomato-based soup. Gazpacho is also delicious with a dollop of plain yogurt or sour cream and chopped chives, as a garnish, instead of the olive oil drizzle.

Susie Wood
Provident Farm
Bivalve, Maryland

65106-05

# OVEN-ROASTED TOMATO SAUCE

2-1/2 lbs. tomatoes, halved
   lengthwise
1 onion, thinly sliced
4 thyme sprigs or 2 T. chopped
   fresh basil

2-3 T. extra virgin olive oil
salt
freshly ground black pepper

Put the tomatoes in a single layer on a baking sheet with the onion and herbs. Drizzle the oil over all, and season with salt and pepper. Bake tomatoes until soft, shriveled, and falling apart, 45 minutes to 1 hour. Remove from oven, remove the thyme branches (if using thyme), and purée with a food processor or pass through a food mill. Taste for salt and season with pepper.

**Recipe Note:** Serve with pasta. Also, use as a dipping sauce for a calzone, as a base for red pizza or as an accompaniment with grilled fish or grilled meat.

Ted McCormack and Wendy Crofts
Willow Pond Community Farm
Brentwood, New Hampshire

# HEIRLOOM TOMATO SALAD

6 vine-ripened heirloom
  tomatoes
1/2 tsp. salt
freshly ground black pepper
flake sea salt
1 tsp. Dijon mustard

1 garlic clove, chopped
1 T. tarragon or white wine
  vinegar
1 T. fresh lemon juice
1/4 c. olive oil
3 T. finely chopped fresh chives

Core the tomatoes and slice them from tip to stem into 1/2 inch slices. Lay the slices on a large plate, sprinkle with 1/2 teaspoon salt and let sit for 15 minutes. Drain any juice that has accumulated on the plate and arrange the slices on a serving platter. Give a few turns of the pepper grinder over the tomatoes and sprinkle with sea salt. Combine the mustard and garlic in a small bowl and stir in the vinegar and lemon juice. Slowly beat in the oil. Spoon the vinaigrette over the tomatoes and sprinkle with chives.

Ted McCormack and Wendy Crofts
Willow Pond Community Farm
Brentwood, New Hampshire

65106-05

# CHUNKY MEDITERRANEAN HERBED TOMATO SAUCE

2 medium onions, diced small
5 garlic cloves, finely chopped
1/4 c. olive oil
3 lbs. tomatoes, peeled, seeded
  and coarsely chopped
3 T. finely chopped fresh basil
3 T. finely chopped fresh
  parsley

1-1/2 T. minced fresh oregano
1-1/2 T. minced fresh thyme
1-1/2 T. minced fresh sage
dash of dried pepper flakes
salt and pepper, to taste

In a large sauce pan, cook onions and garlic in olive oil over moderately high heat for 15 minutes, stirring frequently. Add tomatoes, herbs and red pepper flakes and cook 15 minutes. Stir occasionally. Season with salt and pepper, Serve immediately or refrigerate in a tightly sealed container for up to four days. Sauce also freezes well. Makes 4 cups of sauce.

Karen Vollmecke
Vollmecke Orchards CSA
Brandywine, Pennsylvania

# GRILLED CHEROKEE PURPLE TOMATO SANDWICHES

## (With tapenade)

½ c. imported pitted and chopped kalamata olives or finely chopped black olives
1 small clove of garlic
1-½ tsp. fresh lemon juice
2 tsp. olive oil, divided
freshly ground black pepper

8 slices sturdy rustic-style rosemary or focaccia bread
8 thick slices of Cherokee purple tomatoes, ¼ inch thick
2-½ oz. Gorgonzola cheese, cut into 8-12 thin slices

In a bowl, combine olives, garlic, lemon juice, 1 teaspoon of oil and pepper. Then spread 2 teaspoons of this mixture across 4 slices of bread. Top each of the 4 slices of bread with 2 slices of tomato and 2 to 3 slices of cheese. Then add 2 more teaspoons of mixture to bread stack. Use the other 4 slices of bread to make sandwiches and press together firmly. Heat large skillet until hot. Cook each sandwich over low heat until golden brown on each side. Serve warm.

Bill Brammer III
Be Wise Ranch CSA
San Diego, California

65106-05

# Heirloom tomato salsa

## (A Spanish recipe)

freshly squeezed juice of one lime or lemon
1-2 cloves of fresh garlic, crushed
6-8 green onions, chopped
8 radishes, finely chopped
fresh cilantro, chopped
fresh oregano, minced
a dash of soy sauce

¼ tsp. cumin
¼ tsp. chili powder, cayenne or hot red peppers
4 beefsteak-style heirloom tomatoes (such as Purple Cherokee, Brandywine or Black Krim)
honey
salt

Whisk together lime/lemon juice, garlic, green onions, radishes, cilantro, oregano, soy sauce, cumin, and chili powder. Chop all heirloom tomatoes and add to mixture. Add hot peppers, honey and salt to taste.

**Recipe Note:** The secret to this recipe is to add just enough honey, so that you can taste an underlying sweetness. If the tomatoes are very sweet to begin with, you won't need much honey. This salsa is best served one hour after refrigeration. Serve the salsa with tortilla chips or use it as a condiment.

Marsanne Brammer
Be Wise Ranch CSA
San Diego, California

# Heirloom crostini

12 slices of baguette-style
  bread, ½ inch thick slices
1 garlic clove, peeled and left
  whole
4 oz. goat cheese
12 pieces of zucchini thinly
  sliced or arugula leaves
12 beefsteak-style heirloom
  tomatoes (such as purple
  Cherokee or green zebra), ½
  inch thick

olive oil
sea salt
freshly ground black pepper
freshly snipped basil

Position oven rack to the second from the top level to prepare to broil. Arrange bread on baking sheet; rub with garlic clove and toast both sides until golden. Spread 1 teaspoon of goat cheese across each slice of bread. Top cheese with 1 slice of zucchini and 1 tomato slice. Lightly brush tomato slice with the olive oil and sprinkle with salt and pepper. Broil about 40 seconds or until tomato is warmed. Sprinkle each piece with basil or lay one leaf of arugula across the top of each. Serves 12.

Bill Brammer III
Be Wise Ranch CSA
San Diego, California

65106-05

# STRIPED GERMAN TOMATOES WITH TARRAGON

3 sweet yellow bell peppers
3 large striped German
  heirloom tomatoes
2 T. tarragon vinegar (recipe
  follows)
2 T. olive oil
1 tsp. Dijon mustard

sugar
sea salt
freshly ground black pepper
1/2 tsp. snipped fresh tarragon
  (keep additional sprigs for
  garnish)

Place peppers in a foil-lined baking sheet and broil, turning several times until blistered and blackened. Put peppers in a plastic bag and let cool. Core and skin peppers, cut into quarters and then set aside. Core tomatoes and cut into 1/4 inch thick slices. Using a mixing bowl, whisk together the vinegar, oil, mustard, sugar, salt and pepper. Stir in 1/2 teaspoon tarragon. On a serving platter, place alternate rows of tomatoes and peppers; repeat and then drizzle with dressing. Serves 4.

Tarragon Vinegar

2 c. white wine vinegar
5-7 sprigs of fresh tarragon,
  for use and garnish

1 whole garlic clove, peeled

In a non-metallic pan, heat vinegar almost to a boil. Remove from heat. Add tarragon and garlic clove. Let everything steep until cool. Remove herbs and garlic. If desired, place 2 to 3 sprigs of tarragon into glass bottle or other container with a stopper and pour cooled vinegar over tarragon.

Bill Brammer III
Be Wise Ranch CSA
San Diego, California

# TOMATO SOUP WITH INDIAN SPICES

8 medium tomatoes
3-1/2 c. water
1/2 tsp. butter
1/4 tsp. pepper
1/4 tsp. chili powder
1/2 tsp. cumin

1/4 tsp. ground ginger or fresh
   ginger, minced
1/4 tsp. garlic powder or fresh
   garlic, minced
salt to taste
plain yogurt, for garnish

Cut the tomatoes into quarters. Cover with water. Bring to boil. Cook until tomatoes are tender. Add all other ingredients. Mash tomatoes as needed. Serve hot. Garnish with yogurt.

**Recipe Note:** Simple and tasty! If you are a purist, you can strain to remove tomato skins and seeds.

Jeanine Jenks Farley
Waltham Fields Community Farm
Waltham, Massachusetts

65106-05

# Fresh tomato gazpacho

6 large ripe tomatoes (3 lbs.)
1-1/2 c. tomato juice
1 slice dry bread, broken into
   small chunks
1/4 yellow onion, diced
2 T. lime juice
2 T. olive oil
1 T. white wine vinegar
1 tsp. salt

1/2 tsp. oregano
1/2 tsp. basil
1 garlic clove
1/4 c. cucumber, peeled, seeded,
   and finely chopped
1-2 jalapeño chilies, seeds
   removed and minced
Tabasco, to taste

Seed and finely chop 1 tomato, set aside. Coarsely chop remaining tomatoes. Combine these with the tomato juice, bread, onion, lime juice, oil, vinegar, salt, oregano, basil, and garlic in a blender (may need 2 batches) and process until smooth. Stir in the reserved tomato, cucumber and chilies. Add Tabasco to taste (remember, spice can amplify over time). Refrigerate covered, up to 24 hours to blend flavors. Garnish with your choice of slivered avocado, fresh basil leaves, garlic croutons, thinly sliced radishes or lime wedges.

Solyssa Visalli
Cop Copi Farms
La Grand, Oregon

*"If we make our goal to live a life of compassion and unconditional love, then the world will indeed become a garden where all kinds of flowers can bloom and grow."*

Elisabeth Kubler-Ross

# TOMATO BRUSCHETTA

## Topping

2 medium tomatoes cored and chopped (2 cups)
14 fresh basil leaves, slivered (1-1/2 tablespoons)
1/2 tsp. minced fresh garlic

1 T. olive oil
1 tsp. balsamic or red wine vinegar
1/4 tsp. salt (or to taste)

Mix tomatoes, basil, vinegar, olive oil, minced garlic, salt and pepper in a bowl.

## Bread

1 crusty baguette or country loaf of bread
1 large whole clove of garlic, peeled

olive oil

Preheat broiler on high. Slice baguette into 1/2 inch rounds (or 4 slices of country bread 1/2 inch thick). Lay bread cut side up on a cookie sheet. Brush with olive oil and place under broiler for 1 or 2 minutes until lightly browned; watch carefully to prevent burning. When bread is cool enough to touch, rub the toasted bread with a garlic clove. Adjust salt and pepper in tomato mixture to taste. Top toasted garlic-rubbed bread with tomato topping and enjoy.

**Recipe Note:** Originally from Italy, bruschetta is traditionally a workman's midday snack. Thick slices of country bread are grilled over an open fire, rubbed with a clove of garlic, drizzled with a nice fruity olive oil and sprinkled with sea salt. The different regions of Italy further embellish bruschetta by adding various toppings.

Amy Nichols, Clemson University
Calhoun Field Laboratory Student Organic Farm
Clemson, South Carolina

65106-05

# AN ECLECTIC
# HARVEST

# AN ECLECTIC HARVEST

## WHITE ASPARAGUS WITH COCONUT AND MUSHROOM CREAM

**(This dish is delicious with a glass of red wine!)**

10 mushrooms, sliced
1 T. butter
4 green garlic pieces or 2 garlic
  cloves, chopped
3 sprigs thyme, chopped

1 can of concentrated coconut
  milk
8-10 stems of white asparagus
2 servings of fully cooked rice

In a medium-sized skillet at medium heat, dry sauté the mushrooms until they begin to release their juices. Turn the heat down, push the mushrooms to the edge of the pan, add the butter, garlic and thyme. Cook until garlic is fragrant, quickly mix ingredients in pan together and set aside. In a saucepan, heat the coconut milk at a low temperature, adding the mushroom/herb mixture when warm, set aside. At the same time, peel the asparagus and steam until tender, but still have a little crispness to them. When asparagus is done, serve on a bed of rice, topped with the mushroom coconut cream.

Julie Beaumont-Potter
Fairview Gardens
Goleta, California

# CREAMY BOK CHOY SOUP

1 T. dark sesame oil
3 scallions, cut into large
   pieces
3 cloves garlic, peeled and
   crushed
2 slices fresh ginger 1/4 inch
   thick (use 4 slices maybe 2
   inches long, 1/4 inch thick)

1 lb. bok choy, cut into 2 inch
   sections
1 potato, diced
1 sweet red pepper, diced
   (optional depending on
   season)
3 c. water or broth
salt and pepper, to taste

In a soup pot, heat sesame oil over medium heat. Add scallions, garlic, and ginger. Cook, stirring, two or three minutes until fragrant. Add bok choy, potato, water, salt, and black pepper (red pepper, hot sauce/chili powder) and bring to a boil over high heat. Cover, reduce to low, and simmer 20 minutes or until potato is tender.

**Recipe Note:** Optional add-ins: Asian-inspired hot sauce and/or chili powder, snap peas or snow peas (cut in half) or ground meat. Add snow peas and meat last, if using, and cook until peas are cooked to your liking.

Julia Wiley
Marquita Farm & Two Small Farms
Watsonville, California


# RACHEL'S BURDOCK CHIPS

burdock roots
cooking oil

salt
tamari or soy sauce

Wash and diagonally slice the root into thin chips. Sauté slowly in olive oil in a cast iron skillet until crisp. Salt during the sauté and add a little soy sauce or tamari.

Joel Pitney
Winter Green Farm
Noti, Oregon

65106-05

# CALALLO SOUP

## (Also known as Jamaican Pepperpot Soup)

1-½ lbs. soup meat (any meat of your choice)
½ lb. yams, peeled and chopped
2-½ lbs. calaloo finely chopped (also known as: vegetable amaranth; it is used like spinach)
12 okra, cut in small rings
1 small eggplant, peeled and chopped
1-½ lbs. kale, finely chopped
3 large scallion stalks, finely chopped
1 medium onion chopped
1 garlic clove, crushed
1-2 thyme sprigs
1 whole unbroken green hot pepper
1 lb. shrimp, precooked
½ c. coconut milk

Place soup meat in a large soup kettle with about 4 quarts of cold water. Boil until meat is nearly cooked and add yams. Place all chopped greens and other vegetables except the green pepper in a large soup pot and steam covered until cooked, about 10 minutes. Rub all vegetables through a coarse strainer or colander into soup kettle. Add all seasonings and green hot pepper. Add more boiling water, if needed. Simmer until soup appears to have thickened. Then add shrimp and coconut milk and cook for 5 minutes more.

**Recipe Note:** I asked my student Roberta who is originally from Jamaica for a recipe using calallo. This Pepperpot Soup is a Jamaican tradition. Substitute spinach in place of the calallo for a similar taste. Calallo leaves are delicious stir-fried or steamed. As you might imagine, the calallo plant is very tolerant of the heat. -Julie

Julie Sochacki

# Hearty celeriac bisque

1 celery root (approximately 1 pound), peeled and cubed
2 large potatoes, peeled and cubed
lemon juice
1/2 c. chopped carrots
2 leeks, washed very well and chopped

3 T. olive oil
2 garlic cloves, minced
5 c. vegetable or chicken stock
1/3 c. whipping cream or half and half
freshly ground black pepper, to taste

Place celery root and potatoes in cold water with a few drops of lemon juice. Trim leeks and slice into 1/2 inch rounds. Pour olive oil into a large saucepan. Add leeks and garlic. Cook until leeks are soft and garlic is golden, about 5 minutes. Add stock, celery root, potatoes, and carrots. Bring to a boil. Cover, lower heat and simmer until potatoes are tender, about 30 minutes. Purée in batches in a food processor. Strain through a sieve. Place purée back in pan. Simmer, adding enough cream or half and half to obtain proper thickness. Season with freshly ground black pepper. Serves 4.

Julie Sochacki

65106-05

# CELERY ROOT AND BUTTERNUT SQUASH SOUP

## (Lentils add iron and protein to this autumn soup!)

3 T. butter
1 onion, chopped
1 apple, peeled and chopped
1 small celeriac, peeled and chopped or 1 celery stalk chopped
1 garlic clove
4 fresh sage leaves, minced
1 fresh sprig of thyme
1 qt. puréed squash

1 c. tomato, canned and chopped
2-4 c. stock (to make soup desired consistency)
½ c. lentils, fully cooked
salt, to taste
Optional: roasted red pepper, crushed fresh garlic, capers, or 1 tablespoon of sugar or maple syrup

Sauté onions, apple, celeriac, garlic, sage and thyme in butter. Purée this mixture combined with puréed squash. Heat the squash mixture, tomatoes, stock, lentils, and salt on medium heat. Serves 6 to 8.

**Recipe Note:** Celery root or celeriac works well in this soup!

Lali Hess
Michaela Farm
Oldenburg, Indiana

# CELERY ROOT MASH

## (A great addition to the Thanksgiving table!)

1 celery root, peeled and diced
5 medium red potatoes, washed and peeled
2 large sweet potatoes, peeled and diced

1 c. reduced-fat sour cream
4-6 oz. cream cheese
1 tsp. freshly ground black pepper
1 tsp. garlic powder

Boil potatoes and celery root until tender. Drain and return to pan. Mash mixture. Add cream cheese, sour cream, black pepper and garlic powder. Mash and stir until completely combined. Serve immediately or keep warm until served.

Julie Sochacki

# Fresh Cowpeas

1 lb. fresh cowpeas
2-1/2 c. water
6 slices of crisp bacon,
  crumbled

1 onion, chopped
1 T. bacon drippings
salt and pepper, to taste

Rinse peas, put in medium size saucepan with water. Bring to boil, then reduce heat to simmer. Sauté onion in bacon drippings. When peas are tender (about 30 minutes) drain and add sautéed onion and drippings. Season with salt, pepper, and bacon.

Robbins Hail
Bear Creek Farms
Osceola, Missouri


# Daikon Mashed Potatoes

Equal amounts (50%-50% by
  volume) of daikons and
  potatoes, unpeeled
Any combination and amount
  of olive oil, milk, butter, sour
  cream, yogurt, or cream
  cheese

salt and pepper

Cut daikons and potatoes into 1 to 2 inch chunks. Boil in a large pot of water. Check potatoes and daikons after 10 minutes for tenderness with a long sharp knife. Remove those that are tender to a large bowl, leaving the rest to boil until done. Mash daikons and potatoes together in a large bowl with remaining ingredients.

Eva Worden
Worden Farm
Punta Gorda, Florida

65106-05

# GLAZED DAIKONS
## (Delicious addition to an autumn dinner.)

1-1/2 lbs. daikons, quartered or
   sliced (about 4 cups)
1-1/2 c. unsalted butter
1-1/2 c. pure maple syrup

3/4 tsp. sea salt
freshly ground black pepper, to
   taste

Place the daikons in a sauté pan large enough to hold them without overlap in a single layer. Add the butter, maple syrup, salt, pepper, and enough water to cover the daikons halfway. Turn the heat on high and bring to a boil. Reduce the heat to low, and cover and simmer for 10 minutes. Uncover, raise the heat, and bring to a boil. Boil until the liquid has reduced to a shiny glaze and the daikons are tender. Serves 4.

**Recipe Note:** Letting them reduce as long as possible in the final stage, increases the sweetness. They're great!

Jim Britt
Hannah Creek Farm
Four Oaks, North Carolina

# BAKED ENDIVE (FRISEE)

2 T. butter
1 T. flour
1 c. heavy cream

1 bunch endive
2 oz. Gorgonzola
bread crumbs

Melt the butter in a sauce pan over low heat and stir in flour until a thick paste forms. Slowly add the cream to the flour, stirring constantly to make a simple white sauce. Simmer while cutting the endive in half, rinse, and steam in a double boiler until wilted, about 5 minutes. Arrange endive, cut side up, in a shallow baking dish, and cover with white sauce. Break the cheese into small pieces and sprinkle over sauce, top with bread crumbs, then bake in a preheated oven at 400 degrees for 10 minutes or until lightly browned.

Michael Peroni
Boistfort Valley Farm
Curtis, Washington

# FABULOUS FAVA BEANS
## (A traditional Portuguese recipe.)

2 c. medium-sized shelled fava beans (1 lb. fava beans in the pod will yield one cup of shelled beans)
2 cloves chopped garlic (hardneck types will taste better)

½ lb. Portuguese linguica or Italian sausage
½ c. chopped onion
one small can of tomato sauce (or 2-3 diced tomatoes)

Shell fava beans. Do not remove the cuticles (the skin around each shelled bean). Doing so will remove some of the characteristic flavor of the bean. Boil favas with garlic in just enough water to cover beans, about 10 minutes until skins begin to wrinkle. Meanwhile slice linguica or Italian sausage into rounds. Brown sausage and onions lightly in a skillet to render out some of the fat. If using fresh tomatoes, add the tomatoes to this mixture after removing the fat. Add sausage, onions and tomatoes to the fava beans and simmer together 10 to 15 minutes more. Makes a hearty side dish for about 6.

**Recipe Note:** This recipe can also be made using very young fava beans in the pod (like giant string beans). These will be hard to find and only available early in the season. Chop them into pieces about an inch long and increase cooking times slightly.

Bill Nunes
Contented Acres Produce
Gustine, California

65106-05

# FENNEL & ORANGE SALAD

5 baby fennel bulbs, or 2 large ones

**Dressing**

½ blood orange; seeded (or ⅓ larger orange)
2 tsp. rice wine or cider vinegar
1 T. Dijon mustard

1 T. capers, drained
1 T. chopped parsley

2 tsp. sugar
½ tsp. salt
4 T. olive oil

Trim the stalks from the fennel, cut the bulb in half lengthwise; then cut crosswise into very thin slices. Place in a large bowl with the capers and the parsley. Make the dressing. Cut the blood orange half in small pieces and place in the work bowl of a food processor with the vinegar, mustard, sugar and salt. Process until smooth. With the processor running slowly, pour in the olive oil. Pour over the fennel, toss well and serve.

Julia Wiley
Marquita Farm & Two Small Farms
Watsonville, California

*"To know someone here or there with whom you feel there is understanding in spite of distances or thoughts unexpressed - that can make of this earth a garden."*

*Johann von Goethe*

# FRESH FENNEL BAKED WITH TOMATO SAUCE

1-1/2 lbs. fresh fennel (approx. 2
   medium bulbs)
3 T. extra virgin olive oil
4 garlic cloves, sliced
1 small onion, minced
1 T. dried parsley
1 (28 oz.) can tomatoes,
   chopped
5-6 leaves of fresh basil torn
   into pieces

2 T. chopped fresh thyme
   leaves
1/2 tsp. fennel seeds
salt and pepper, to taste
1 tsp. sugar
2 T. grated Pecorino Romano
   cheese

Cut the stalks from the fennel and discard. Cut the bulbs in half and then cut into 1 inch think chunks. Place the fennel into a large pan and cover with cold water. Cover and bring to a boil. Reduce heat and simmer for about 7 to 8 minutes. Fennel should be fork tender. Drain and place fennel in a single layer in casserole dish. Meanwhile in a saucepan sauté the garlic and onion in the olive oil until the onion is translucent. Stir in the dried parsley. Add the tomatoes, basil, thyme, fennel seeds, salt and pepper. Bring to a fast boil uncovered for about 15 minutes stirring so it doesn't pick up. Add sugar during the last five minutes. Pour enough of the tomato sauce to cover the fennel. Sprinkle with the grated cheese and bake at 425 degrees for about 15 minutes.

Julie Sochacki

65106-05

# Kohlrabi vegetable stew

2-3 medium kohlrabi bulbs with greens
1-2 T. olive oil
1 large onion, chopped
3 medium carrots, cut into ¾ inch chunks
3 medium potatoes, cut into ¾ inch chunks
1 c. peeled and chopped tomatoes
4 c. vegetable broth
1 bay leaf
½ tsp. dried oregano
1 tsp. salt
pepper
1 T. Dijon mustard
½ tsp. molasses

Separate leaves from kohlrabi bulbs. Peel bulbs and cut into large chunks. De-rib leaves and cut into thin strips. Set aside. Heat oil in a large pot over medium heat. Add onions and sauté for several minutes. Add kohlrabi bulb chunks, carrots, potatoes, tomatoes, broth, bay leaf, oregano, salt, pepper, molasses and mustard. Turn up heat to medium-low, cover and simmer for about 15 minutes or until vegetables are not quite tender. Add kohlrabi leaves and simmer uncovered for another 10 minutes or until vegetables are fully cooked.

Kay Fernholz
Earthrise Farm
Madison, Minnesota

# Fruity kohl-slaw

1-2 medium kohlrabies, peeled and grated
1 c. cabbage shredded
1 small apple, cored and sliced
½ c. raisins or currants
½ c. seedless grapes
2 tsp. olive oil
½ c. apple cider

Combine the first 5 ingredients in a large bowl. Lightly drizzle oil and cider over the top. Gently toss and refrigerate for several hours to let the flavors mellow. Toss and serve.

Kay Fernholz
Earthrise Farm
Madison, Minnesota

# KOHLRABI WITH HONEY BUTTER

8 small kohlrabi, peeled & cut into 1/4 x 1/4 x 1 sticks
2 medium carrots, peeled & cut into 1/8 x 1/8 x 1 strips
2 c. chicken broth
2 T. chopped parsley
1/2 tsp. shredded lemon peel
2 T. lemon juice
2 T. honey
1/4 tsp. fresh black cracked pepper
2 T. butter

In a medium saucepan cover and cook kohlrabi and carrots with chicken broth for 6 to 8 minutes or until crisp tender. Add parsley, lemon peel, lemon juice, honey, pepper and butter. Toss lightly and serve. Serves 8.

Kelly Saxer
Desert Roots Farm CSA
Queen Creek, Arizona

65106-05

# KOHLRABI GRATIN

4-6 kohlrabi with leaves
1 T. butter or olive oil
1 clove garlic or ½ garlic scape
   thinly sliced
2-3 T. sliced green or bulb
   onion

3-4 c. stock
3-4 T. flour
salt and pepper, to taste
2 oz. sharp cheddar or other
   strong cheese, grated

Remove greens from kohlrabi and set aside. Cut off roots and tops of kohlrabi and trim off fibrous outer layer. Slice into ¼ inch slices or cube into ½ inch pieces. Wash greens. Remove stems using a knife to make v-cuts in the leaves. Stack several leaves together, roll like a cigar, and thinly slice into strips ⅛ inch to ¼ inch wide. Repeat. In a large pan heat 4 quarts water to a boil. Add leaves. Test for tenderness and bitterness. Cook until leaves are on the verge of losing their bright green color. Remove and drain. In a large sauté pan, heat butter or oil. Sauté garlic and onion for 2 minutes. Remove, set aside. Add 3 cups of stock to pan, bring to a low boil. Add kohlrabi bulb pieces. Cook until tender crisp. Remove from pan. Remove 1 cup of stock and into it stir flour. Add back to stock in sauté pan. Salt and pepper to taste. Stir to prevent lumps. Add onion, kohlrabi, and kohlrabi leaves. Coat with sauce. Add ½ to 1 cup more stock if mixture is too dry. Adjust seasoning if necessary. Transfer to a greased 2 to 3 quart baking dish. Top with grated cheese. Bake at 375 degrees until cheese is brown, approximately 15 to 20 minutes.

Anna Barnes
Prarieland CSA
Champaign, Illinois

# CHESAPEAKE BAY OKRA

okra, washed and trimmed with
 a quarter or half-inch of
 stem, keep the whole okra
 intact

vegetable oil
old bay seasoning or seasoning
 of your choice

Roll okra in a small amount of oil, and then sprinkle with seasoning. Spread the okra onto a pan and broil until tender.

**Recipe Note:** I love okra so much that I'll eat it raw. But even when I'm inclined to cook, speed and ease are critical. This recipe is so fast that I can cook it in the toaster-oven for just twice the time it takes to toast bread! -Carrie

Robert and Carrie Vaughn
Clagett Farm
Upper Marlboro, Maryland


# OKRA PILAU

2 c. thinly sliced okra
3 bacon slices, diced
1/2 c. chopped green pepper
1/2 c. chopped onion
3/4 c. long grain rice, uncooked
2 c. chicken broth

1 (16-oz.) can tomatoes, well
 drained and chopped or 3
 fresh tomatoes, peeled,
 quartered and seeded
1 tsp. salt, or to taste

Sauté okra and bacon until lightly browned. Add green pepper and onions and continue cooking until vegetables are tender. Add rice, chicken broth, tomatoes, and salt. Bring to a boil. Stir once, cover, reduce heat and simmer 15 minutes or until rice is tender. (If using converted rice, increase the chicken broth to 2-1/4 cups and the cooking time to 25 minutes.) Fluff lightly with fork and serve.

Jolinda Hamilton
Hamilton Farms
Clinton, Arkansas

65106-05

# Okra and Potato Ragout

2 lbs. okra
¼ c. olive oil
1 large onion, finely sliced
2 large potatoes, cut in
  quarters

3 c. water
2 T. parsley, finely chopped
2 large ripe tomatoes, cubed
juice of one lemon
salt and pepper, to taste

Clean and wash the okra well. Cut in half, lengthwise, if large. Drain and salt. In a large saucepan heat oil and sauté onion until golden. Add potatoes and 2 cups of water. Simmer covered for 25 minutes. Add 1 cup water, okra, parsley and tomatoes. Cook gently for an additional 15 minutes. Increase heat and cook for 15 to 20 minutes, uncovered. Five minutes before cooking is complete, add lemon juice. Shake saucepan (do not use a spoon). Let stand for 8 minutes before serving.

Kelly Saxer
Desert Roots Farm CSA
Queen Creek, Arizona


# Fried Okra

16 oz. okra
¼ c. all-purpose flour
¼ c. corn meal
⅛ tsp. salt

¼ tsp. Cajun seasoning or
  black pepper
1 egg
¼ c. vegetable oil

Wash okra and cut off the tips and stem ends. Cut the pods crosswise into slices about ¼ inch thick. Combine flour, cornmeal, salt and pepper in a medium bowl. In another bowl, beat the egg. Dip okra into the egg, coating on all sides, and then dredge in the flour mixture, making sure to completely cover the okra. Heat the vegetable oil in a skillet over medium-high heat. Add okra and fry until brown, about 10 minutes, depending on thickness. Flip to make sure the okra is crisp and browned on both sides. Drain on paper towels before serving.

Kelly Saxer
Desert Roots Farm CSA
Queen Creek, Arizona

# Sautéed pea green tips
## (Dou Miao-pronounced "dough meow")

2 T. sesame oil
3 T. finely chopped garlic
8 c. fresh pea green tips

¼ c. chicken broth
2 tsp. cornstarch
salt, to taste

Cook oil and garlic in a wok until tender. Add and cook the pea green tips until ready to wilt. Then add chicken broth, cornstarch and salt. Sauté until greens are wilted and broth has started to thicken. Serve over rice or eat by itself.

**Recipe Note:** This was one of my favorite dishes in China! -Sarah

Sarah Wu-Norman
Merck Forest & Farmland CSA
Rupert, Vermont

# Radish leaf patties

2 c. fresh radish leaves,
   chopped
2 small or 1 medium carrot,
   peeled and shredded
1 small purple onion or
   scallions, chopped
minced garlic to taste

1 tomato, diced
2 eggs, beaten
salt to taste
1 T. wheat flour
1 T. vegetable oil
1 T. margarine

In a mixing bowl combine first 7 ingredients. Add flour and toss to combine. Heat oil and margarine in skillet over medium heat. Pour radish leaf mixture by spoonfuls into skillet. Cook until golden, turning once. Enjoy with your favorite salsa. Makes about 8 patties.

Elaine Granata
Granata Farms
Denver, Colorado

65106-05

# Scapes Pesto

⅛ lb. scapes
¼ c. olive oil

½ c. grated Parmesan cheese

Chop scapes into ¼ inch sections. Blend scapes with olive oil. Place the blend in a bowl and stir in Parmesan. Use on bread, potatoes, pasta, over cauliflower or as a dip.

Elaine Granata
Granata Farms
Denver, Colorado

# Fried Zucchini Flowers

12 zucchini flowers
1 c. flour
2 large eggs
¼ c. cold water
¼ c. Pecorino Romano grated
  cheese

½ tsp. salt
½ tsp. black pepper
1 tsp. baking soda
canola oil, for frying

Clean and wash the flowers removing the stems and the small green spikes at the base. Gently press the flowers between paper towels to remove excess water. Place flour on a piece of wax paper. Dredge the flowers into the flour shaking off any excess. In a bowl combine the 2 large eggs, water, grated cheese, salt, pepper and baking powder. Meanwhile heat the oil in a frying pan. Dip the flowers into the egg mixture and fry on both sides until golden brown. Change the oil between batches if needed. Drain on paper towels. Serve immediately.

**Recipe Note:** I have fond memories of gardening with my grandmother and picking the zucchini flowers for this unusual treat! -Julie

Julie Sochacki

65106-05

# PRESERVING THE HARVEST

# PRESERVING THE HARVEST

## HOME CANNING CAUTION

Due to the technical nature of home canning, and the impact upon food safety that improper techniques can have, novice canners must become educated on the art of canning and on the use of proper equipment for safe home canning. This book is not intended to educate the novice home canner. Resources that fully explain canning procedures are available.

**Resources**

The Ball Blue Book is a comprehensive how-to book on food preservation. Also, the USDA Food and Nutrition Information Center provides accurate, reliable information for home canners.

*"Go confidently in the direction of your dreams! Live the life you've imagined. As you simplify your life, the laws of the universe will be simpler."*

*Henry David Thoreau*

# HOT CHILLY DILLY

8 lbs. trimmed yellow beans
(can use green too)
16 heads of dill
16 cloves of garlic
4 tsp. cayenne pepper

4 tsp. mustard seed
4 tsp. crushed red pepper
10 c. vinegar (5% acidity)
10 c. water
1 c. canning salt

Pack beans lengthwise into hot jars. To each quart add 1/2 teaspoon each of the cayenne, mustard seed and crushed red pepper. Also add to each quart-sized jar, 2 cloves of the garlic and 2 heads of dill. Bring water, vinegar and salt to a boil. Pour hot liquid into jars leaving 1/4 inch head space. Remove air bubbles and screw on caps. Process 10 minutes in boiling water bath. Makes 8 quarts.

Bonnie Biller
St. Martin de Tours Organic Farm
Palermo, Maine

# PICKLED GREEN BEANS

4 lbs. green beans
1-3/4 tsp. crushed red pepper
3-1/2 tsp. mustard seed
3-1/2 tsp. dill seeds

7 garlic cloves
5 c. water
5 c. white vinegar
1/2 c. canning salt

Wash beans and remove ends. Cut beans into 2 inch pieces, divide among several pint jars. Put 1/4 teaspoon of red pepper, 1/2 teaspoon mustard seeds, 1/2 teaspoon dill seeds, and 1 clove of garlic into each of the jars. Combine water, vinegar, and salt and bring quickly to a boil. Pour boiling liquid over beans, leaving 1/2 inch in headroom. Process in a boiling water bath for 10 minutes.

Jolinda Hamilton
Hamilton Farms
Clinton, Arkansas

65106-05

# PICKLED OKRA

small, whole okra
garlic
hot pepper
mustard seeds

dill seeds
vinegar
canning salt

Pack 6 pint jars with small whole okra. Put 1 to 2 cloves of sliced garlic, 1 pod of hot pepper, 1/2 teaspoon mustard seeds, 1/2 teaspoon dill seeds into each jar. In a saucepan combine 3 cups of water, 2 to 2-1/2 cups of vinegar, and 4 tablespoons of canning salt. Bring to a boil and pour over okra leaving 1/2 inch headroom. Process in a boiling water bath for 5 minutes.

Jolinda Hamilton
Hamilton Farms
Clinton, Arkansas

# JALAPEÑO JELLY

## (CAUTION: Wear gloves when handling jalapeños!)

3/4 lb. whole jalapeño peppers
6 c. sugar
2 c. cider vinegar

2 (3-oz.) pouches liquid pectin
10 drops of food coloring,
(optional)

Wash and half peppers, lengthwise. Remove stems and seeds. In a food processor or blender, blend peppers and half of vinegar until smooth. In a large saucepan, combine sugar, pepper mixture, and remaining vinegar. Bring mixture to a full, rolling boil, stirring constantly. Remove from heat. Stir in coloring. Skim foam, if necessary. Immediately fill half-pint jars, leaving 1/4 inch head space. Seal and process in boiling water bath for 5 minutes.

Jolinda Hamilton
Hamilton Farms
Clinton, Arkansas

# RED TOMATO JAM

ripe firm tomatoes, free of
   blemishes
granulated sugar

lemon juice
half of a cinnamon stick or a
   piece of lemon rind (optional)

Choose some ripe, firm tomatoes that are free of blemishes. Remove stalks and plunge them into boiling water for 1 minute. Remove from water and peel. Cut into small pieces, and then steep for two hours with their weight of granulated sugar and the juice of two lemons per 2-1/4 pounds tomatoes. Put the mixture in a pan and bring to a boil. Cook very gently until the syrup reaches the jelling stage, about 1 to 1-1/4 hours. Process in jars using standard canning techniques, or store in tightly sealed glass jars in the refrigerator for up to one month. If desired, push a cinnamon stick or lemon rind down in the center of each jar before sealing.

Carole Koch
Green Earth Institute Farm
Naperville, Illinois

# LISA MAASEN'S SWEET PICKLES
## (Wonderful, delicate pickles!)

8 qts. fresh baby cucumbers,
   thumb-sized
1/2 c. pickling salt
4 c. vinegar

8 c. sugar
1 tsp. turmeric
1 T. celery seed
1 T. pickling spices

Wash cucumbers carefully; place in crock. Pour boiling water over them. Let stand overnight. Drain and repeat pouring boiling water over the cucumbers for 6 days. On the 7th day, drain and sprinkle with pickling salt. Cover with boiling water. Let stand overnight. On the 8th day, drain and prick cucumbers with fork. Combine vinegar, sugar, turmeric, celery seed and pickling spices. Heat and pour over cucumbers each morning for two more mornings. Pack in jars, filling with boiling syrup. Quickly add caps and rings and allow to seal.

Harriet Kattenberg
Seedtime & Harvest
Hull, Iowa

65106-05

# PICKLED HOT PEPPERS

4 qts. peppers
1/4 c. sugar
2 T. horseradish
2 c. water

10 c. vinegar
pickling salt
carrots, onions, garlic
(optional)

Wear rubber gloves. Clean peppers and cut 2 slits in each pepper. Cut carrots into slices and onions into wedges. Combine sugar, horseradish, water and vinegar in large pan. Simmer for 15 minutes. Pack carrots, onion, garlic and peppers into hot jars leaving 1/4 inch head space. Add 1 tsp. pickling salt to top of each pint jar and 2 tsp. to each quart. Heat pickling liquid to boiling and pour over peppers. Install lids and rings and tighten.

Harriet Kattenberg
Seedtime & Harvest
Hull, Iowa

# PRESERVED LEMONS
## (BItter, sour, sharp and tangy!)

whole Meyer lemons, preferably
  organic
more lemons for juicing

salt
glass jar with non-metal, tight
  sealing lid

Add 1 to 2 tablespoons of salt into the bottom of the jar. Cut lemons, but don't completely separate into quarters. Generously salt insides of lemons, and press into jar. (It's okay if they separate.) Compress all cut and salted lemons into a jar so that no space is left. Add fresh lemon juice to cover all lemons. Add 2 more tablespoons of salt. Cover. Shake this beautifully brilliant jar daily. Let it sit as a decorative piece on your counter. Mark your calendar for 6 weeks, and then enjoy for up to 1 year in the refrigerator.

**Recipe Note:** These lemons are worth the effort! The flavor when added to stews, lentil dishes, chicken, lamb, potato salad, or Greek salad, just to name a few, is fantastic.

Deborah Hildebrandt
Be Wise Ranch CSA
San Diego, California

# "CURING" VEGETABLES

## (Dip with Italian bread and don't forget the vino!)

vegetables of your choice: green
  beans, artichokes, eggplant,
  peppers, pearl onions, etc.
white vinegar

extra virgin olive oil
fresh mint
salt
garlic cloves

Place cleaned and cut vegetables inside the jar along with salt, garlic, and mint (about 2/3 full). Continue to fill with white vinegar, until the jar is 3/4 full. Fill the rest of the jar with olive oil, and slightly shake or stir to blend ingredients and vegetables. Place a piece of round linen over the top of the outside of the jar before screwing on the cap or just cover the linen with plastic and use a thick rubber band to hold it securely (the cloth keeps mold and mildew from building). Keep jar for about two months in a cool storage area and it will allow the veggies and ingredients to blend and take on a delicious flavor that will make a great side dish as an addition to an appetizing table spread.

**Recipe Note:** If curing eggplant, peel the eggplant and slice paper thin. If curing green beans, clip off ends. If curing pearl onions, peel first. If curing artichoke hearts, clean and cut hearts in half.

Mary Cannavo
Sophia Garden
Amityville, New York

# SQUASH RELISH

6 c. chopped squash (yellow)
6 c. chopped zucchini
2 c. chopped onions
1 T. canning salt

3 c. white vinegar
4-1/2 c. sugar
2 tsp. celery seed
2 tsp. mustard seed

Chop squash and onions. Sprinkle with salt. Let stand 1 hour. Drain and pack into pint jars. Bring vinegar, sugar and seeds to a boil. Pour into jars and seal. Process in boiling water bath for 20 minutes.

Jolinda Hamilton
Hamilton Farms
Clinton, Arkansas

65106-05

# CUCUMBER RELISH

2 qts. cucumbers, chopped
2 c. chopped green peppers
2 c. chopped red pepper
1 c. chopped onion
1 T. ground turmeric
½ c. pickling salt

2 qts. water
1-½ c. brown sugar
1 qt. white vinegar
2 (3-½ inch) cinnamon sticks
1 T. mustard seed
2 tsp. allspice

Combine cucumbers, peppers, and onions. Sprinkle with turmeric. Dissolve salt in 2 quarts of water. Pour over vegetables and let stand 3 to 4 hours. Drain. Cover vegetables with cold water and let stand 1 hour. Drain thoroughly. Combine sugar and vinegar in a large stainless steel saucepan. Tie cinnamon sticks, mustard seed, and allspice in a cheesecloth bag. Add to vinegar mixture and bring to a boil. Pour over veggies. Cover and let stand overnight in a cool place. Remove spice bag. Bring mixture to a boil. Fill pint jars and seal. Process in boiling water bath for 20 minutes.

Jolinda Hamilton
Hamilton Farms
Clinton, Arkansas

# TOMATILLO JAM

2 qts. fresh tomatillos
6 c. white sugar
2 T. lemon juice

1 container liquid pectin
6 cinnamon sticks

Remove paper skin from tomatillos and rinse. Place in a food processor and mash. Measure 4 cups of the mash into a large pot. Stir in the sugar and lemon juice. Bring to a full rolling boil over high heat, and boil hard for 1 minute, stirring constantly. Remove from heat, and stir in pectin at once. Skim off any foam with a large metal spoon. Sterilize jars and lids in boiling water for at least 10 minutes. Take turns with skimming foam, and stirring the berry mixture for 5 minutes to let it cool slightly. Before ladling into hot sterile jars, add one cinnamon stick to each jar. Leave 1/4 inch head space then seal jars with lids and rings. Makes 6 one pint jars.

Jackie Good
RC Organic Farm CSA
Lenox, Michigan

# PEAR JAM

4 c. pears, peeled, cored and
   finely chopped
2 T. lemon juice

1-3/4 oz. pectin
5 c. sugar

In a large saucepan stir together pears, lemon juice, and pectin. Bring mixture to a rolling boil, stirring constantly. Quickly add sugar. Bring to another rolling boil and boil hard for one minute, stirring constantly. Remove from heat and skim foam if necessary. Fill 1/2 pint jars leaving 1/4 inch headroom. Seal and process in a boiling water bath for 5 minutes.

Jolinda Hamilton
Hamilton Farms
Clinton, Arkansas

65106-05

# WILD MUSHROOM SOUP BASE
## (A great base for so many soups and stews!)

3 T. olive oil
3 garlic cloves, chopped
2 shallots, chopped
2 leeks, white and light green
    parts thinly sliced
2-3 lbs. of your favorite fresh
    mushrooms, sliced
1/4 c. sherry wine

1-1/2 T. fresh thyme
1 bay leaf
2 T. fresh parsley
1 tsp. sea salt
2 tsp. fresh ground pepper
2-4 c. vegetable or chicken
    stock

In a 4 quart stock pot, add olive oil, shallots, garlic, and leeks. Stir fry until the garlic is golden and the shallots and leeks are translucent, about 3 minutes. Add mushrooms and sherry. Cook the mixture covered for about 10 minutes or until the mushrooms are tender. Add all other ingredients. Allow the mixture to cool slightly. Discard the bay leaf and pour the mixture into the blender and purée. Pour back into the stock pot. After the base has cooled, pour it into either small covered containers for use in mushroom soup later or into ice cube trays. Freeze. (Ice cube trays are great to add mushroom flavor to a recipe). If frozen in ice cube trays, transfer cubes to a freezer bag, for later use.

Julie Vitale
Jupazza Specialty Products/Vitale Farms CSA
Rochester Hills, Michigan

# Zucchini Soup

## (Freeze and save for winter months!)

1 large zucchini (4-½ cups
  grated)
½ c. chopped onion
3 c. chicken stock
½ c. butter
4 T. flour

1 tsp. salt
pepper, to taste
2 c. milk
shredded cheese such as
  cheddar (optional)

Cook zucchini, onion and stock. Remove. In skillet, melt butter, stir in flour and cook until bubbly. Add milk and seasonings. Add to cooked vegetables and heat. Top with shredded cheese.

**Recipe Note:** When freezing, do not add milk and cheese. Add the milk and top with cheese when reheating the soup to eat.

Dave Chirico & Matt Ferut
Two Guys Farm
Reynoldsville, Pennsylvania

# Denison Farm's Basil Pesto

## (Freezes for one year!)

3 c. tightly-packed basil leaves,
  picked off the stem
½ c. pine nuts or walnuts
½ c. grated Parmesan or
  Romano cheese

3-4 garlic cloves, cut coarsely
½-¾ c. olive oil

Buzz all ingredients except the olive oil in a blender or food processor. Add the olive oil in a stream while processing until it forms a smooth paste. (Scrape down the sides.) For short-term storage, spoon into a narrow jar, cover with oil, and refrigerate for up to a week. For long-term storage, freeze in ice cube tray and store cubes in a freezer bag. Lasts 1 year.

Justine and Brian Denison
Denison Farm
Schaghticoke, New York

65106-05

# Salsa Verde

## (Freezes well!)

| | |
|---|---|
| 1-½-2 lbs. tomatillos | 2-3 garlic cloves |
| 1-4 hot peppers | 1 tsp. salt, or salt to taste |
| 1 small onion, peeled | 2-4 T. chopped cilantro leaves |

Remove husks from tomatillos and boil in a small amount of water, covered, for a couple of minutes (until they change color). Cool slightly and drain off most of the water. Pour in blender and add remaining ingredients. Blend until smooth. If not tart enough, add a squeeze of lemon juice or tablespoon of white vinegar. Use on nachos, quesadillas, enchiladas, or as a tortilla chip dip.

**The salsa tastes great in**
  **Chicken Enchiladas Verde**

Fill lightly fried (but still pliable) corn tacos with shredded, cooked chicken seasoned to taste with oregano, ground cumin, garlic salt, a little minced onion and shredded Monterey jack cheese. Roll up and arrange in glass baking dish, top with more shredded cheese and microwave or heat in oven until cheese just melts. Pour warm salsa verde over top and serve.

Trish Mumme
Garden Patch Produce CSA
Alexandria, Ohio

*"Opportunity is missed by most people because it is dressed in overalls and looks like work."*

*Thomas A. Edison*

# RATATOUILLE
## (The variations are endless!)

1 medium eggplant, peeled
2 small zucchini
1 medium green bell pepper,
  chopped
1 medium onion, finely chopped
2 medium tomatoes, each cut
  into fourths

$\frac{1}{4}$ c. olive oil
1-$\frac{1}{2}$ tsp. salt
$\frac{1}{4}$ tsp. pepper
1 garlic clove, crushed

Cut eggplant into $\frac{1}{2}$ inch cubes. Slice zucchini into $\frac{1}{4}$ inch slices. Cook all ingredients in a 12-inch skillet over medium heat, 10 to 15 minutes, stirring occasionally, until zucchini is tender. Makes about 6 servings.

**Recipe Note:** For a new twist on this ratatouille, add sliced red potatoes, carrots and beets. Double the recipe, it freezes well!

Les Roggenbuck
East River Organic Farm
Snover, Michigan

# SWEET AND SOUR TOMATILLO SAUCE

$\frac{1}{2}$ lb. sweet white onion,
  quartered
$\frac{1}{2}$ lb. tomatillos, husked and
  quartered

1 T. vinegar
2 T. sugar
$\frac{1}{2}$ c. water
2 T. cornstarch

Purée onion, tomatillos, vinegar, sugar, and $\frac{1}{4}$ cup of water in a blender. Transfer to a sauce pan and cook over medium heat for 10 minutes. In a small bowl combine the cornstarch and $\frac{1}{4}$ cup of cold water. Add to the tomatillo mixture and stir well. Cook for an additional 2 to 3 minutes until the sauce thickens slightly. Serve hot or cold with fried chicken, pork, or beef or with a stir-fried vegetable dish. This tomatillo sauce will keep refrigerated for about two weeks.

Jinny Cleland
Four Springs Farm
Royalton, Vermont

65106-05

# FRESH TOMATO MARINARA SAUCE
## (Freeze and save for a quick pasta dinner!)

5 lbs. fresh tomatoes
1/4 c. extra virgin olive oil
8 garlic cloves, minced
1 tsp. dried parsley
3 T. chopped fresh parsley
1 tsp. dried basil

1/2 tsp. fresh ground black
  pepper
salt to taste
1 tsp. sugar
10 fresh basil leaves

Put the fresh tomatoes in a pot of boiling water for about 10 seconds until the skin can be easily peeled off. Discard the skins. Cut tomatoes in pieces and place in blender in batches. Turn blender to chop for about 10 seconds. Put fresh tomatoes in sauce pan and boil uncovered for about 15 minutes. In the meantime place olive oil in another sauce pan and gently sauté the garlic. Do not let garlic turn brown. Add the fresh parsley, dried parsley and dried basil. Then add the fresh tomatoes, black pepper and salt to taste. Cook over medium heat for about 20 minutes uncovered. Add sugar and torn fresh basil leaves to the sauce. Cook for another 5 minutes.

**Recipe Note:** This amount of marinara sauce will perfectly accompany one pound of your favorite pasta. Sprinkle with freshly grated Parmigano Reggiano cheese.

Julie Sochacki

# TART CRANBERRY, CARAMBOLA, ORANGE SAUCE

1 bag cranberries
2 carambolas, chopped
2 oranges or tangelos, chopped

$\frac{1}{3}$-$\frac{1}{2}$ c. sugar, Splenda, or honey

Place cranberries in a saucepan, together with chopped carambolas and chopped oranges (or tangelos). Add $\frac{1}{3}$ to $\frac{1}{2}$ cup sugar or Splenda, or an equivalent amount of honey. Boil gently together, stirring to keep from burning, until thickened. Pour into a dish and chill. Serve as a spread on bread with cream cheese, or as an accompaniment to turkey, ham or chicken. This keeps very well in the refrigerator.

Margie Pikarsky
Redland Organics' Bee Heaven Farm CSA
Redland, Florida


# FIESTA SALSA

7 c. peeled, cored, seeded, chopped tomatoes
2 c. seeded, chopped banana peppers (sweet)
1 c. sliced green onion
$\frac{1}{2}$ c. roasted, peeled, chopped, Anaheim peppers

$\frac{1}{2}$ c. chopped jalapeño peppers
$\frac{1}{4}$ c. minced cilantro
3 cloves garlic, minced
1 T. minced fresh marjoram
1 tsp. salt
$\frac{1}{2}$ c. cider vinegar
2 T. lime juice

Combine all ingredients in a large sauce pot. Bring mixture to a boil. Reduce heat and simmer 10 minutes. Ladle hot salsa into hot jars, leaving $\frac{1}{4}$-inch head space. Adjust two-piece caps. Process 15 minutes in a boiling-water canner. Yield: about 4 pints.

Harriet Kattenburg
Seedtime & Harvest
Hull, Iowa

65106-05

# SWEET ENDINGS

# SWEET ENDINGS

## APPLE CAKE
(Quick and easy.)

1-³/₄ c. sugar
1 c. canola oil
3 large eggs
2 c. flour
1 tsp. baking soda

¹/₄ tsp. salt
4 large apples (cored, peeled
  and sliced)
1 tsp. cinnamon
¹/₂ c. walnuts

In 9 x 13 pan, blend together sugar and oil. Add eggs, flour, baking soda and salt. Mix well. Add apples, cinnamon and walnuts. Mix well. Bake at 350 degrees for 45-60 minutes.

Carl & Mary Anne Castle
Maple Creek Farm
Yale, Michigan

# Hot Apple and Cranberry Compote

2 c. fresh or frozen cranberries
3-1/2 c. peeled and cubed tart
　apples

1 tsp. lemon juice
1 c. granulated sugar
1/2 tsp. cinnamon

Topping

1/2 c. soft butter
2/3 c. packed brown sugar

1-1/3 c. oats
1 tsp. cinnamon

Combine cranberries, apples and lemon juice in a greased 2 quart casserole dish. Mix sugar and cinnamon together and sprinkle over the top of the fruit. Combine dry topping ingredients in a medium bowl. Cut butter and mix into dry mixture to make a crumbly topping. Sprinkle topping over fruit. Bake for 1 hour at 350 degrees. Delicious with turkey, as an ice cream topping, or served alone topped with whipped cream. Serves 6 to 8.

Pamela Pour
Maple Creek Farm
Yale, Michigan

65106-05

# COUNTRY APPLE COBBLER
## (Shredded cheddar makes this cobbler rustic!)

1-1/3 c. sugar, divided
1/4 c. water
2 T. quick-cooking tapioca
1/4 tsp. ground cinnamon
6 c. thinly sliced and peeled
  tart apples
1 c. all-purpose flour
1 tsp. baking powder

1/4 tsp. salt
1/3 c. melted butter or
  margarine
1/4 c. milk
1-1/2 c. shredded cheddar
  cheese
1/2 c. chopped walnuts
whipped topping (optional)

In a large saucepan, combine 1 cup of sugar, water, tapioca, and cinnamon. Bring to a boil over medium heat, stirring occasionally. Remove from heat; stir in apples until coated. Pour into a greased 8 x 8 inch baking dish; set aside. In a small bowl, combine the flour and baking powder, salt and remaining sugar. Stir in butter and milk, just until mix is moistened. Fold in cheese and walnuts. Sprinkle over apple mixture. Bake at 375 degrees for 30 to 35 minutes or until filling is bubbly. Serve with whipped topping.

Jolinda Hamilton
Hamilton Farms
Clinton, Arkansas

# New England Autumn Apple-Cranberry Pie
## (A true taste of autumn!)

4 apples, peeled and cut
1/4 c. cider or water
1-1/2 c. sugar
3 T. cornstarch
1/4 tsp. salt
nutmeg, to taste

cinnamon, to taste
2-1/2 c. cranberries
2 T. grated orange rind
3 T. butter
2 unbaked pie crusts

Place apples and cider or water in a medium sauce pan. Cook on medium heat for 5 minutes. Add sugar, cornstarch, salt, nutmeg, cinnamon, and cranberries. Cook until a few berries pop. Take off heat and add orange rind and butter. Place crust in a pie plate, add filling, and top with second crust. Add slits in pie crust to vent. Protect edges of crust from burning with foil rim. Bake at 350 degrees for 40 minutes or until done.

**Recipe Note:** I have been making this pie from my friend Kathy Talbert for years. It's a great way to use apples in the fall, and the results are delicious! -Valentine

Valentine Doyle
Holcomb Farm CSA
West Granby, Connecticut

# Yellow squash pie

1/2 stick butter
1-1/2 c. shredded squash
1/2 c. sugar
3 eggs

1 T. flour
1 tsp. lemon flavoring
1 tsp. coconut flavoring
1 unbaked pie shell

Mix all ingredients together and pour into an unbaked pie shell. Bake at 350 degrees for 30 to 35 minutes.

Jeni Galvin
Sunshine Gardens
Charlottesville, Virginia

65106-05

# DOUBLE-CHOCOLATE ZUCCHINI CAKE

2-1/2 c. flour
1/2 c. cocoa
1 tsp. baking soda
1/2 tsp. salt
1/2 c. butter
1-1/2 c. sugar

1/2 c. oil
2 eggs, beaten
1 tsp. vanilla
1/2 c. milk
2 c. grated zucchini
6 oz. chocolate chips

Combine flour, cocoa, soda, and salt. Cream butter and sugar; beat in oil, eggs, and vanilla. Add the milk while alternating with dry ingredients to the butter mixture. Pour into greased 9 x 13 baking pan and sprinkle chips over top. Bake at 325 degrees for 35 to 45 minutes.

Genevieve Stillman
Stillman's Greenhouses & Farm Stand
Lunenburg & New Braintree, Massachusetts

# CHOCOLATE ZUCCHINI CAKE

1/2 c. good-quality cocoa
1/2 c. oil
1/2 c. butter
1-3/4 c. sugar
2 eggs
1 tsp. pure vanilla
1 tsp. baking soda
1/2 tsp. baking powder

1/2 tsp. salt
1 T. lemon juice
1/2 c. milk
2-1/2 c. flour
2 c. grated zucchini
1/4 c. chopped nuts
1/4 c. brown sugar
1/4 c. chocolate chips

Mix well cocoa, oil, butter, sugar, eggs, and pure vanilla. Add baking soda, baking powder, and salt. In a measuring cup mix lemon juice with milk and add to batter. Gradually add flour, then grated zucchini. Pour into greased 9 x 13 cake pan. Mix chopped nuts, brown sugar, and chocolate chips. Sprinkle this mixture on top of batter. Bake at 350 degrees for 30 to 40 minutes.

Anne Morgan
Lakes & Valley CSA/Midheaven Farms
Park Rapids, Minnesota

# ZUCCHINI BLONDIES

## (Zucchini and chocolate, a great combination!)

1 c. flour
1 tsp. baking powder
1 tsp. baking soda
1/2 tsp. salt
1-1/4 c. brown sugar
1/3 c. butter
2 eggs

1 tsp. vanilla
1 c. shredded and squeezed dry
zucchini
1/2 c. semi-sweet chocolate
chips
1/2 c. coarsely chopped walnuts
(optional)

Lightly grease a square 8 x 8 baking pan. In a bowl, mix the flour, baking powder, baking soda, and salt. In another bowl, mash together brown sugar and butter until light and fluffy. Beat eggs and vanilla into the sugar mixture. Gradually combine flour mixture with sugar mixture. Then stir in zucchini, chocolate chips and walnuts. Pour batter into the pan. Bake at 350 degrees for about 30 to 40 minutes. (After 25 minutes, if top is browned, cover loosely with tin foil, and continue to bake until done.) Cool, cut and enjoy!

Franz Rulofson, College of the Redwoods
Sustainable Agriculture Farm
Shively, California

65106-05

# Maple pound cake
## (Great with fresh berries!)

4 sticks butter
3 c. maple syrup, at room
  temperature
6 eggs

2 tsp. vanilla extract
4 c. flour
1 T. baking powder
½ tsp. salt

Butter and flour two loaf pans or one 10 inch tube pan. Sift the dry ingredients together. Cream butter with an electric mixer on high speed until light and fluffy. Whip in maple syrup until light and fluffy. Add eggs, one at a time, beating until light and fluffy. Add vanilla. Fold dry ingredients, mixing well, but not too much. Spread batter into buttered/floured pans and bake at 350 degrees for 50 to 60 minutes or until a toothpick inserted in the center comes out clean. Allow to cool before slicing.

Sara Schlosser
Sandiwood Farm
Wolcott, Vermont

# Sugar on snow
## (A Vermont tradition!)

1 qt. pure Vermont maple syrup      packed snow or well-crushed ice
½ tsp. butter

Use a large pot; heat syrup and butter. Watch pot and turn heat down if it threatens to boil over. When a candy thermometer reaches 234 degrees, remove from heat and cool slightly. Test by spooning a tablespoon of thickened syrup over the snow; If the syrup sits on top of the snow and clings to a fork like taffy, it's ready. Pour in "ribbons" over snow packed in bowls. Traditionally served with sour pickles and plain doughnuts. Serves about 10.

**Recipe Note:** It takes 40 gallons of maple sap to boil down to or evaporate into 1 gallon of maple syrup! -Sara

Sara Schlosser
Sandiwood Farm
Wolcott, Vermont

# Merck Forest Maple Cream Pie

1 (14-oz.) can sweetened
  condensed milk
2/3 c. pure maple syrup
dash of salt
1 (9 inch) graham cracker crust

1/2 pt. whipping cream
1/4 c. confectioners' sugar
1/4 c. salted chopped pecans,
  toasted
1 tsp. cinnamon

In saucepan, combine condensed milk, syrup, and salt. Bring to full rolling boil over low heat, stirring constantly. Cool to room temperature. Pour into crust. In mixing bowl, beat cream on high slowly adding confectioners' sugar until stiff peaks form. Spread over pie. Sprinkle with mixture of nuts and cinnamon. Cool for 3 hours or until filling is set.

Linda McLenithan
Merck Forest & Farmland Center CSA
Rupert, Vermont

# Merck Forest Maple Cookies

1 c. plus 2 T. flour
1/2 tsp. baking soda
1 stick butter (8 tablespoons),
  softened
1/2 c. sugar (substitute with
  maple sugar, also known as
  Indian sugar)

1/2 c. light brown sugar
1 egg
1/4 tsp. salt
1-1/2 tsp. vanilla
1 c. chopped maple sugar candy

Whisk together flour and baking soda and set aside. Beat butter and sugars on medium speed until fluffy. Then add egg, salt and vanilla to creamed mixture. Stir in flour mixture and maple sugar candy. Drop 2 inches apart on cookie sheet and bake one sheet at a time at 375 degrees for 8 to 10 minutes. Let cool for 2 minutes on sheet before moving to cooling rack.

Sarah Wu-Norman
Merck Forest & Farmland Center CSA
Rupert, Vermont

65106-05

# FRESH PUMPKIN PIE

3 large eggs (preferably organic)
2 c. fresh pumpkin purée (organic)
2/3 c. sugar (for extra sweetness, increase sugar to 3/4 cup)
1/2 tsp. vanilla extract
1/2 tsp. sea salt

1-1/4 tsp. ground cinnamon
1/2 tsp. ground ginger
1/8 tsp. ground cloves
10-11 oz. evaporated milk (comes in a 12 oz. can) (low-fat evaporated milk will not work well)
1 pastry pie shell
freshly whipped cream

Gently beat eggs on low with electric mixer or with wire whisk. Add pumpkin purée and blend well. Add sugar, vanilla, salt and spices and mix well. Finally, add evaporated milk. Pour pie mixture into prepared uncooked pastry shell. Protect edges of crust from burning with foil rim. Bake at 375 degrees for 40 minutes. Remove foil and bake an additional 20 minutes (total cooking time is roughly one hour). Check doneness by inserting knife until it comes out almost clean. Once pie is totally cool, store covered in refrigerator. Serve with freshly whipped cream. Serves 6 to 8.

**Recipe Note:** Puréed fresh pumpkin has a high water content so this is a slightly different recipe. As you mix the pumpkin pie with your fresh pumpkin you will notice that it is thinner than you may be accustomed to seeing, if you normally use canned pumpkin. -Pamela

Pamela Pour
Maple Creek Farm
Yale, Michigan

*"When the sun rises, I go to work. When the sun goes down, I take a rest, I dig the well from which I drink, I farm the soil which yields my food, I share creation, Kings can do no more."*

*Chinese Proverb, 2500 BC*

# "NICOLE SMITH" BUTTERNUT SQUASH PIE

1 butternut squash
2 eggs, beaten
1/2 c. flour
1/3 stick margarine
1/4 c. sugar

honey
1 tsp. vanilla extract
1 pie crust
nutmeg and/or cinnamon

Cut squash vertically in half. Scoop out seeds. Set skin side on lightly greased cookie sheet and roast at 350 degrees for 45 minutes. Scoop out flesh and let cool in a mixing bowl. Mix squash with two eggs, flour, margarine, sugar, a squirt or two of honey, and vanilla extract. Pour into pie crust and sprinkle with nutmeg and/or cinnamon. Protect edges of crust from burning with foil rim. Bake at 350 degrees for about 45 minutes.

**Recipe Note:** I named this pie after my friend Nicole who gave me the recipe while in graduate school in New York. -Mara

Mara Hutt-Tiwald
Green Earth Institute Farm
Naperville, Illinois

65106-05

# TOFU PUMPKIN PIE

3 eggs, lightly beaten
6 or 12 oz. silken firm tofu
1 small can evaporated milk or sweetened condensed milk
1 (15-oz.) can pumpkin purée (2 cups)
1 c. brown sugar

½ tsp. vanilla
1-2 tsp. cinnamon
1-2 tsp. ground ginger
¼-½ tsp. nutmeg
¼ tsp. cloves
¼ tsp. allspice
salt

Mix eggs and sugar in a bowl, then add milk, pumpkin, tofu, salt and spices. Blend all ingredients until smooth. Pour into unbaked crust. Protect edges of crust from burning with foil rim. Bake at 400 degrees for 45 minutes or until crust is golden brown and filling is firm. Remove from oven, cool on baking rack and serve warm.

### Vinegar-Egg Pastry

1 egg
1 tsp. vinegar
5 T. water

3 c. flour
1-¼ c. shortening
2 tsp. salt

Mix egg, vinegar and water. Sift dry ingredients; cut in shortening with a pastry cutter or pair of butter knives. Add egg mixture, then roll out balls of dough to fit pie plate/pan. Makes 3 crusts.

**Recipe Note:** This pie-filling recipe is very tolerant of variations of tofu and milk amounts. Also, even though premade pie crusts have become the standard, this simple recipe produces a pie crust of exceptional texture, allegedly because of the vinegar. The vinegar does not adversely affect the flavor of the pie.

Annaliese Franz & Jared Shaw
Waltham Fields Community Farm
Waltham, Massachusetts

# SWEET POTATO PIE
## (A delicious alternative to pumpkin pie!)

2 lbs. sweet potatoes, peeled
1 stick butter, softened
1 c. sugar
2 T. brown sugar
5 oz. can evaporated milk
2 eggs, beaten
1 tsp. lemon juice

1 tsp. vanilla extract
pinch of salt
1 tsp. cinnamon
1/4 tsp. nutmeg
2 unbaked pie shells
whipped topping

Boil sweet potatoes until tender. Mash sweet potatoes with butter. Stir in sugars, milk, eggs, lemon juice, vanilla, salt, cinnamon, and nutmeg. Pour into shells, protect edges of crust from burning with foil rim and bake at 425 degrees for 15 minutes. Then reduce heat to 350 degrees and bake for 35 minutes (or until inserted knife comes out clean). Cool and top with whipped topping.

Shelley Squier & Mike Donnelly
Squier Squash & Donnelly Farms
North English, Iowa

65106-05

# CANDY ROASTER PIE

1-¼ c. fresh candy roaster
  squash purée
¾ c. sugar
½ tsp. salt
¼ tsp. ground ginger
1 tsp. ground cinnamon
1 tsp. all-purpose flour

2 eggs, lightly beaten
1 c. undiluted reduced-fat
  evaporated milk
2 T. water
½ tsp. vanilla extract
1 pastry shell, unbaked (9 inch)

Combine squash, sugar, salt, spices, and flour in a mixing bowl. Add eggs and mix well. Add evaporated milk, water, and vanilla and mix well. Pour into pastry-lined pie plate. Protect edges of crust from burning with foil rim. Bake at 400 degrees for 15 minutes. Reduce heat to 350 degrees and bake about 35 minutes longer or until center is set.

**Recipe Note:** If you're lucky enough to get candy roaster squash, try making this pie. You'll never go back to pumpkin again!

Carole Koch
Green Earth Institute Farm
Naperville, Illinois

# YUMMY WALTHAM BUTTERNUT SQUASH MUFFINS

## (Freeze for school lunches!)

2-1/2 c. flour
1 c. sugar
4 tsp. baking powder
1 tsp. cinnamon
1 tsp. nutmeg
1/2 tsp. salt

1/4 c. butter
2 eggs
1-1/2 c. butternut squash,
   cooked and well-drained
3/4 c. milk
1 c. raisins

Sift together the first 6 ingredients. Cut in the butter until mixture resembles corn meal. Beat eggs and add squash, milk, and raisins and stir. Add wet ingredients to dry, just enough to mix. Pour into standard-sized greased muffin tins. Bake 350 degrees for 30 to 35 minutes. Makes 24 muffins.

**Recipe Note:** The Waltham butternut squash, with its distinctive bell shape, was developed at the University of Massachusetts Agricultural Field Station in Waltham, Massachusetts. The farm continues to grow the Waltham Butternut on the site where it was first bred, along with many other vegetables, for hunger relief programs and for our CSA members.

Friends of Waltham Fields Community Farm
Waltham, Massachusetts

65106-05

# CEREAL FRUIT PIE
## (With mint ice cream!)

### Pie Shell

1 c. flour
½ tsp. salt
⅓ c. oil
2 tsp. warm water
 (approximately)

nutmeg, cinnamon or sugar; for
 extra flavor

Mix all ingredients. Roll into a ball and then roll out dough to fit pie plate/pan. Bake until lightly browned. Let pie shell completely cool.

### Filling

berries (choose your favorite)
apples, sliced

1 c. cereal or granola

Add fruit and cereal or granola into the cooled pie crust.

### Ice Cream

fresh mint
1 c. milk

1 c. farm fresh cream
1 c. sugar

Place fresh mint in a blender or processor with milk. Add this to an ice cream maker with fresh cream and sugar. Follow ice cream maker's instructions. Top the ice cream over your berry pie.

Susan & Jonathan Trumpetto
Piedmont Organics CSA
Linden, Virginia

# SPRING HARVEST STRAWBERRY SORBET

## ("Streak" the sorbet with melted chocolate!)

4-4-1/2 c. fresh picked
  strawberries
1/4 c. water (spring water
  preferable)
1/2 c. sugar

1/4 tsp. sea salt
1/4 tsp. fresh squeezed lemon
  juice
1 local farm fresh egg white
  (optional)

Rinse, hull and pat dry the fresh picked strawberries. In a saucepan combine the water and sugar and salt. Cook on moderate heat until the sugar and salt are dissolved creating a simple syrup. Place prepared strawberries, lemon juice and simple syrup in a blender and blend until smooth. (If you prefer, you may strain the seeds now.) Mixture will taste slightly sweeter than when frozen. Cover and refrigerate until cold.

**Freezing the Sorbet**

Pour cold base into your ice cream maker and freeze according to your ice cream maker's directions. When partially frozen, you may add the optional egg white. This helps to stabilize, emulsify and preserve the texture of the sorbet, if you plan to keep it in your freezer to eat over a few days. (Raspberries work great too.) Yields about 1 pint.

**Recipe Note:** My husband Matt and I, own the Bent Spoon, a specialty ice cream shop in Princeton, New Jersey, using local ingredients. We have such special memories of picking baskets full of strawberries and eating them in every conceivable way. This sorbet captures their fresh-picked essence and is so very SPRING! -Gabrielle

Gabrielle Carbone
Honey Brook Organic Farm CSA
Pennington, New Jersey

65106-05

# FINNISH BERRY RICE

1 c. heavy cream
¼ c. sugar
2 c. raspberries, blueberries or
   halved strawberries

2-3 c. cooked rice, chilled
fresh mint leaves

Beat the cream until soft peaks form. Gradually add the sugar and beat until stiff. Fold the cream and add 1 cup of the berries into the rice. Spoon into a serving dish and top with the remaining 1 cup of berries and the mint leaves.

Sara Waldron
Grindstone Farm
Pulaski, New York

*"To be the agent whose touch changes nature from a wild force to a work of art is inspiration of the highest order."*

*Bob Rodale, 1962*

# CHEESECAKE WITH MIXED BERRY GLAZE

## Cheesecake

4 (8-oz.) pkgs. cream cheese, brought to room temperature
1-1/2 c. sugar
3 T. cornstarch
3 T. all-purpose flour
4 eggs, brought to room temperature

1 tsp. vanilla
1-1/2 tsp. lemon juice
1 stick butter, melted, and slightly cooled
1 pt. sour cream, brought to room temperature

Using a heavy mixer, mix cream cheese, sugar, cornstarch, flour and eggs for 10 minutes. Add vanilla, lemon juice, melted butter, and sour cream. Mix 5 minutes more. Butter sides and bottom of a 9 inch spring form pan. Pour cream cheese mixture into pan. Bake at 325 degrees for 1 hour. Then shut off the oven and keep the cheesecake in place for an additional 2 hours. Place on cooling rack, and carefully scrape around the perimeter of the pan with a butter knife to loosen. Refrigerate until ready to serve.

## Berry Glaze

2 pt. fresh berries, washed and dried well

1 small jar of strawberry jelly

Cut the strawberries into smaller pieces. Keep smaller berries whole. Dry berries and place in a bowl. Heat jelly on stove stirring with spoon until melted. Pour hot jelly over the berries and combine. Let cool for 10 minutes. Release sides of springform pan and place cheesecake on a platter. Top with glaze before serving.

**Recipe Note:** My aunt introduced me to this cheesecake many years ago. I've tried other cheesecake recipes, but this is the creamiest and most delicious! -Julie

Julie Sochacki

65106-05

# FRESH FARM MUFFINS
## (The variations are endless!)

1-1/2 c. whole-wheat pastry flour
(or all-purpose flour)
1 c. wheat germ, toasted or raw
3/4 c. brown sugar
1/2 tsp. salt
2 tsp. baking powder
1 tsp. baking soda
2 tsp. cinnamon
1 tsp. nutmeg
1/8 tsp. ground clove or allspice
2 eggs, lightly beaten
(substitute: 1/3 cup of soy
milk for 2 eggs)

1-1/3 c. buttermilk (as
substitutes: add a teaspoon
of vinegar to regular milk or
soy milk)
1/3 c. canola oil or butter,
melted
2 c. shredded yellow squash
1 c. shredded zucchini
1 c. shredded carrot
1 c. chopped walnuts or pecans

Mix all dry ingredients in a bowl: flour, wheat germ, brown sugar, salt, baking powder, baking soda, and spices. Then mix all wet ingredients in a second bowl: eggs, buttermilk, oil or butter, and vegetables. Combine the wet and dry ingredients with a few swift strokes. Use a rubber spatula to stir the batter from the bottom and sides of the bowl. Eliminate pockets of flour, but leave lumps in batter, so do not beat. Stir in walnuts or pecans. Scoop the batter into 12 to 16 greased muffin tins. Bake at 375 degrees in the upper third of the oven until browned and well risen, about 25 minutes.

**Recipe Note:** This basic buttermilk muffin recipe can be easily modified. Use different amounts of fresh vegetables or even fresh or dried fruits, sweetened coconut and chocolate chips. For a higher protein variation, replace part of the wheat germ with quinoa, amaranth or soy flour.

Annaliese Franz & Jared Shaw
Waltham Fields Community Farm
Waltham, Massachusetts

# 100% KONA COFFEE AND COFFEE CAKE

## Coffee

**1 T. 100% Kona coffee per cup**     **1 c. pure water per cup**

A truly great cup of coffee can be made with certified organic, freshly roasted 100% Kona coffee. Store it sealed, but not in the freezer and use it soon for best taste. Grind it just before you brew it, coarser for a French press and fine for espresso. Delight in the delicious, complex, mellow flavor.

## Coffee Cake

3 c. flour
1 c. sugar
1 tsp. cinnamon
3/4 tsp. nutmeg
1/2 tsp. all spice
3/4 c. butter (1-1/2 sticks)

1-1/4 c. brewed 100% Kona coffee
3 tsp. baking powder
1/2 c. macadamia nuts (raisins, almonds, walnuts)

Sift together flour, sugar, spices. Cream butter into dry mix, setting aside 1 cup as topping. Add coffee, baking powder and nuts to rest of dry mix. Mix well, and pour into an oiled 8 inch x 8 inch pan. Sprinkle with topping mixture (add 1/2 cup chopped nuts, if desired). Bake at 375 degrees for 25 to 30 minutes.

**Recipe Note:** Coffee Cake is not just to eat with coffee, it should have coffee in it!

Melanie & Colehour Bondera
Kanalani Ohana Farm
Honaunau, Hawaii

65106-05

# LEMON BASIL CAKE
## (Any fresh basil will work in this unique cake!)

2-1/2 c. cake flour
2-1/2 tsp. baking powder
1/2 tsp. salt
1/2 c. butter
1-1/2 c. sugar
2 eggs

1/4 c. chopped lemon basil
1/4 c. chopped lesbos basil
2 T. finely chopped lemon peel
1 tsp. vanilla
1 c. plus 2 T. buttermilk

Grease a 9 x 13 cake pan. Combine the first three ingredients. Mix next five ingredients in separate bowl. Alternating with the buttermilk, mix all ingredients together. Bake at 375 degrees for approximately 40 minutes or until toothpick inserted in center comes out clean. Top with your favorite fruit.

**Recipe Note:** Lesbos basil is also known as Greek columnar basil.

Rusty & Claire Orner
Quiet Creek Herb Farm
Brookville, Pennsylvania


# RASPBERRY MUFFINS

1-3/4 c. flour
3/4 tsp. salt
1/3 c. sugar
2 tsp. baking powder
1/4 c. butter

2 eggs
3/4 c. milk
1 c. raspberries, rinsed well and
    dried

Mix flour with salt, sugar, and baking powder. Melt butter. In a separate bowl, beat eggs and add melted butter and milk. Make a well in center of flour mixture and add liquids, stirring until almost blended. Quickly stir in raspberries. Spoon into greased or paper-lined muffin tins. Bake at once at 400 degrees for 20 minutes.

Anne Morgan
Lakes & Valley CSA/Midheaven Farms
Park Rapids, Minnesota

# RHUBARB BARS

### Crust

1-½ c. flour                        1 c. butter
8 T. powdered sugar

Stir together flour and sugar. Cut in butter. Pat this mixture in a greased 9 x 13 pan and bake at 350 degrees for 10 to 15 minutes, until set but not brown.

### Filling

3 eggs                              ¾ c. flour
2-¼ c. sugar                        3 c. finely diced fresh rhubarb

Beat together eggs, sugar and flour. Stir in rhubarb. Pour this mixture over the hot crust and bake at 350 degrees for 40 minutes until set.

Mary Pat Klawitter
Klawitter CSA
Euclid, Minnesota


# ELLEN'S MOM CELE'S OLD-FASHIONED PEAR CAKE

1 c. cane sugar                     1 tsp. baking powder
½ c. unsalted butter                ¼ tsp. sea salt
2 eggs                              6 small ripe but firm pears,
1 c. whole-wheat pastry flour          leave on skin, core and cut
1 tsp. cinnamon                        into quarters

Cream sugar and butter. Beat eggs well and mix into creamed sugar mixture. Add flour, baking powder, and salt. Pour into buttered and floured 8 x 8 x 2 baking pan. Place fruit on batter in sections, skin side up. Bake for 50-60 minutes at 350 degrees.

Ellen Lane
Future Fruit Farm
Ridgeway, Wisconsin

65106-05

# INDEX OF RECIPES

## AN ECLECTIC HARVEST

## PRESERVING THE HARVEST

## SWEET ENDINGS

# How to Order

Get additional copies of this cookbook by returning
an order form and your check or money order to:

**Julie Sochacki**
**P.O. Box 333**
**New Hartford, CT  06057**
**www.farmcookbook.com**

✁ - - - - - - - - - - - - - - - - - - - - - - - - - - - - - - - - - - - - - - - - - - - - - - - - - -

Please send me _____ copies of **One United Harvest** at
**$15.95** per copy and **$4.00** for shipping and handling per
book. Enclosed is my check or money order for
$_____.

Mail Books To:

Name _____

Address _____

City _____ State _____ Zip _____

✁ - - - - - - - - - - - - - - - - - - - - - - - - - - - - - - - - - - - - - - - - - - - - - - - - - -

Please send me _____ copies of **One United Harvest** at
**$15.95** per copy and **$4.00** for shipping and handling per
book. Enclosed is my check or money order for
$_____.

Mail Books To:

Name _____

Address _____

City _____ State _____ Zip _____

65106-ds